Both Eyes Open and Both Eyes Shut

Corwin Johnson

Library of Congress Cataloging-in-Publication Data
Author Corwin Johnson
Anthony KaDarrell Thigpen,
Publisher
Literacy in Motion Publications

Both Eyes Open and Both Eyes Shut

ISBN: 978-0-9904440-6-0

1. Christians - Religious Life/Self-Help
Printed in the United States of America

Published by
Literacy in Motion
PO BOX 7186
Chandler, AZ 85246
posttribune@hotmail.com
KaDarrell@sbcglobal.net

DEDICATION

Carrie L. Brown
(My Grandmother)

I love you. We all miss you and love you dearly. You may not be physically present with us, but you will always be loved and never be forgotten.

Content

INTRODUCTION

"'Wisdom is supreme; therefore get wisdom. Thought it cost all you have, get an understanding" (Proverbs 4:7).

Supreme: Final; ultimate: so wisdom is final, it's the ultimate.
Wisdom: good judgment, learning, knowledge, clear thinking, experience.
Understanding: the power to think and learn, a specific interpretation.
Now let's say this scripture again.

Good judgment and clear thinking is of ultimate importance, therefore get knowledge. Though it may cost all you have, gain a specific understanding about your life!

All too often, most people are looking in the right and wrong directions at the same time. But most of the time we are looking in the wrong direction! We see what we want to see and hear what we want to hear. And most of the time, we fail to understand the end result of both directions that we are looking! The things we see, hear, and speak are leading us to everlasting life, but where do you plan to spend eternity? To be honest, most of the time our eyes are shut to the direction of everlasting life, and open to the direction of everlasting death! Now if everlasting death is not your direction, with all do respect, I'm not speaking to you! *"But when Jesus heard it, he replied, those who are strong and well (healthy) have no need of a physician, but those who are weak and sick. Go and learn what this means." I desire mercy (that is, readiness to help those in trouble) and not sacrifice and sacrificial victims. For I came not to call and invite (to repentance) the righteous (those who are upright and in right standing with God), but sinners"* (Matthew 9:12-13).

A lot of us are very sick, and we don't even know how sick we are. We just think we have viruses that will go away with time. But spiritual sickness just don't go away like a common cold, you have to put in work in order for this type of sickness to leave the body. You need to activate faith that is deep inside your spirit to get rid of these symptoms. This kind of sickness is not just going to go away because you're a nice person, because you put a smile on your face, or frown which ever one you do the most. This type of sickness is not just going to go away because you go to church every Sunday. What are you getting from going to church every Sunday? You first need to realize that you are sick. Most of us know we are sick but we don't want to be cured. We'd rather complain all the time about how sick we are; what kind of sickness is that? And I don't mean telling someone "I'm sick," much rather always complaining about things going on in your life. When you repeatedly complain about your job, you'll probably lose it. When you repeatedly complain about your children, they have a greater chance of being disrespectful or going to prison. Everyday we see what happens to people that complain about money – they stay broke. Even when people have more than enough, they complain about what they can't get at the moment. We fail to tithe or give offerings, but we steady want God to keep giving to us above and beyond. I can keep going... I've heard people complaining about somebody else's children but what type of grades are your children getting in school? Even worse, people complain about their husbands or wives, and we wonder why the enemy attacks our marriages. Stop complaining about your spouse and pray for them. Love them with all your heart, because know that when you are talking about them you are only talking about yourself. And then there are those that complain about somebody else's husband or wife, but where is your spouse? If your relationship is great, try to help the next couple. Give them marriage-strengthening pointers instead of talking about them. It makes you look foolish, whether you want to believe it or not, and stop complaining about the lack in your life. If you are a complainer, don't worry about having anything more than what you have, because if you can't deal with lack, than what will you do if he gives you more. So, keep complaining about your situation instead of giving praise. See where that will take you. Instead of complaining about what somebody else has, stop worrying about that. Stop comparing yourself with your brother, your sister, your uncle, your aunt, your cousin, your church members, your co-workers and your so-called friends. At the end of the day stop worrying about what others are doing, because you don't know what someone has done to get what they have! You don't know what others had to go through to get where they are. And if you are not willing to do those things or make those sacrifices, then don't expect those results. Complaining all the time is a sign of someone being spiritually sick. We can all use some spiritual healing regardless of who or where we are in life. I know some people will say, "I'm good with where I'm at in life," but be true to yourself. I'm telling the truth, because either you are this person or you know somebody like this. We wonder why some people can't see the path in front of them. Unfortunately, we are too busy concerning ourselves with issues that have nothing to do with us. If you're in love with another man's wife you are sick. Did you think that's something normal to be involved with another man's wife, come on, man! If you are in love with another woman's husband you are also sick. I can hear some women saying, "Well if she was taking care of him like she should be, he wouldn't be with me at all. Evidently, I'm doing something that she's not doing, and it's not my fault that a married man is in love with me." But is he going to leave her? Is he planning a future with you, or is he lying to you, or can you tell the different? Sometimes we can be so sick that we become delusional. Catch me later with "Why Am I So Comfortable Living In My Sins" on more about this type of behavior. Now if we can't love our own family members that have done nothing to us, or even if they have offended us, we have to learn about the cure of "forgiving!" Forgiveness cures a lot of the sickness that many of us have. Sometimes one doesn't realize that the kingdom of God is at hand. We wait until things start going wrong in our lives. All of a sudden, we begin to realize that at any moment my number can be called. One of the worst feelings that we can experience is *Not Knowing* what to feel. So many people don't know what's going on with their health, marriage, children, and finances. I know many of you have never experienced this way of living! After the *Not Knowing* people usually get to a place of being ready to die? Am I prepared to see God? Did I have my house in order, and I'm not talking about my literal house with a roof. I am not talking about that kind of house; I'm talking about the house of self! Right now is a good time to start asking self, "Do I have my spiritual house in order?" "Am I in right standing with God?" "Am I doing what is required of me?" The life that you lived in the flesh will be over! Now moving forward, although you went to church your whole life, you didn't live by the words that you were hearing. All that time you thought going to the *House of Prayer* was enough and everything else would take care of itself. You tell yourself and other people God knows my heart. *"The heart is deceitful above all things, and desperately wicked: who can know it"* (Jeremiah 17:9)? And that is what God tells us. That is God's message for those of us who claim to love Him, but disregard His Word by living reckless lifestyles. Religion, relationship and holiness are more than lip service. Most of the time that is all some of us are doing, giving God lip service. We are not living worthy of the call by being faithful. The Bible says, *"Faith without works is dead."* That is what our lip service is most of the time. I always heard that being holy is not a religion, but a lifestyle. It's how you live for God that will determine your access to heaven – or not! So if you have both eyes open and both shut; what form of afterlife are you seeing!

Welcome to *Both Eyes Open and Both Eyes Shut*. I pray that something in this book will open your eyes to some things that you may have never paid attention to. I hope it enlightens you in some form or another, and that you will be inspired spiritually. The first volume of my *Both Eyes Open and Both Eyes Shut* series will be the self-entitled headliner. The second volume will be *"Why Am I So Comfortable Living In My Sins"* and the third volume will be *"Win, Lose, No Draw,"* dealing with spiritual warfare. I would like to thank you for picking up this edition of my book. I pray that you will find it within yourself to follow me in this journey to try to save souls and see God's people prosper, live holy and saved. If nothing else, I believe it will plant a seed, because that's all any of us can do. We plant the seed, another person waters it, and God gives the increase. I just want to play my part in the process. I would like to thank God, who is the head of my life, for giving me the spiritual insight to not only hear the things that he has been given me, but to put it in written form. So, I give God all the glory and honor, thank you Jesus. I want to give a special thanks to my wife, Molly Johnson, for supporting me in my endeavors; for recognizing the Lord and in life, and for being by my side through it all. You put up with me when I was going through challenges, and I thank you for it all. You are truly my better half and I love you. I want to thank my mother and father, both of whom I would bounce my thoughts off of from time to time, whom I love dearly and wouldn't trade them in for anything in the world, I love you for loving me first. May God bless you and continue to prosper you. I would like to tell my children that I love them, and I especially hope that some things in this book will help them live God-filled lives. More than anyone or any persons, I want to see you all succeed and be all you can be in God. I love you with all my heart. Thanks to my parents, Steve and Samella Johnson. I want to thank my little brother Montell and his family. Thanks brother for believing in me and for giving me advice from time to time about life in general, I love you brother. Special gratitude to my children, Cory, Darrion, Jaelenn, Corshaunta, Paige, Jacoby and Jeremiah Johnson. I would also like to thank LaTonya Archie, my cousin, for her encouragement and warm words, and for her prayers and for being an extra set of eyes for me as I continue to go through this journey. Words can't express the gratitude I have for what you have done for me in my life, and in my spiritual walk, I thank you cousin. You already know, as one advances the other goes as well, love you. I would also like to thank Carol Sims and Terrie Hill for being two of my biggest supporters and encouraging me to keep going in the direction that God was taking me. I thank both of you for taking time out of your days to read my material and for your feedback. Thank you and may God bless you in all that you do. And last but not least I want to thank my entire family, with special emphasis to Carolyn, Dion, Petey, Shantelle, Cherry, Tre' and G' for staying by my side while I went through this journey that God has put me on. I thank my friends and my co-workers for listening to my theories and inspiring me to write. And I would like to thank all my brothers and sisters in Christ. I extend a special thanks to brothers Gino, Darren, Nolan, and Bo. I would like to thank my graphic designer, my friend and my brother in Christ, Antwone Whiteside, Sr. And I would like to thank everyone that has helped me to get *Both Eyes Open and Both Eyes Shut* to God's people. I thank you all and may our Lord and Savior bless you. I love you and I thank you from the bottom of my heart – I am truly filled with gratitude. And again, I would like to thank the Most High God for using me in this hour to try and deliver his word in the way that he has given it to me. I thank *him* for his everyday mercy and grace. I thank *him* for using a "donkey" like me! You'll get it later. And to transition from my thanks, I want to thank two men that have had a huge influence in my spiritual life; my spiritual fathers, Pastor Scott Jefferson and Pastor Roy Hill, I thank you both for your teachings and for your love and support. I thank God for allowing our paths to cross. Thank you and I love you. I want to thank everyone who has supported Corwin (Moneyway) Johnson, and for those who will support me in the future, God bless you all. I would also like to thank my very first pastor; the-late Pastor Benjamin Holmes, for over 50-years on the wall, may you rest in peace.

Chapter 1

LISTEN TO THAT DONKEY TALK

"Then the Lord opened the eyes of Balaam, and he saw the angel of the Lord standing in the way and his sword drawn in his hand: and he bowed down his head, and he fell flat on his face" (Numbers 22:31).

You're about to see that before God opened Balaam eyes he opened the eyes of the donkey first. We all know the other expression for a donkey. God opened the eyes of the *donkey* that Balaam was riding. Had the donkey not seen the angel of the Lord, the angel would have killed Balaam. Actually the sole purpose of the angel was to kill Balaam. So, this book I am your host, Cory Johnson, a.k.a. the donkey. God has opened my eyes in this hour and in this season to gain wisdom and understanding. Now that I've been enlightened, I am to go out to His chosen people and spread the Word. Most importantly, that the world might be saved and blessed through the blood of his son Jesus Christ! So, God is sending me out to help pull the scales off some of your eyes, so that He might open your spiritual eyes. Now, for my brothers and sisters in Christ that are already living a saved and holy lifestyle, I thank you for picking up this book. Now there are some things that God wants us to see, but we're just not ready to see them yet! And sometimes we need people to take us to some places to see things that we never would have seen. Otherwise, we'd continue to walk around blindly.

I'm just an average person and I don't know why God began talking to me and have me writing this book. This is certainly something that I have never done before. But regardless of not knowing the reason why, all I can say is that I have just been obedient to the Voice of God, last 16-

years that he has been speaking to me about *Both Eyes Open and Both Eyes Shut.* During the last 16-years the voice would come and go. I'm learning that when God gives you an assignment, no matter how difficult it is to accomplish, the assignment remains unchanged! But we must wait on God to confirm His will. We must wait to see if this is really what He is telling us to do. We should seek wise counsel. Without proper guidance we find ourselves going in circles. Now I see why I had to repeatedly read about the children of Israel. What should have took no more than 3-4-years, took me 16-years to accomplish. It took me 16-years to hearken to the Voice of the Lord. Here comes the donkey with a message from the Lord! C. J. Moneyway your eyes has been shut long enough. Honestly, for some of us, our eyes have been shut for so long we don't even realize that the death angel is on the same road we're traveling. It is my understanding that no man can recover if he/she dies in the midst of sins. People think that sin is not that big of a deal. Some might even say, "I'm still living aren't I?" God has forgiven me of my sins in the past regardless of what I have done for real you know me and God, we good!" But we will get more into the "sin issue" in the 2nd volume *"Why Am I So Comfortable Living In My Sins!"*

There is a word for when someone consciously plans out and commits a murder, it's called premeditated murder. Premeditated murder is a crime of wrongfully and intentionally causing the death of another human being. After rationally considering the timing and/or method of murder, in order to increase the likelihood of success, or evade detection or apprehension. Well, because this is true, then there is such a thing called premeditated sin! And the wages of sin is death also.

Now some might say, "How could there be such a thing called premeditated sin?" I know myself better than anyone, and I know I have been guilty of premeditated sin on many occasions! You know on that Tuesday, just pick a Tuesday, any year-any month. I know I'd already made up my mind on that Thursday I was going to commit a particular sinful act. Remember, I knew that Tuesday that I was going to sin on Thursday. I didn't care about the consequences either. You can believe that. You know as long as I was getting what I wanted at the time the consequences didn't matter. And just like many of us today, we're still murdering people, and some have even committed suicide. Come on brother, you knew on Monday you were going to go and do a drive by on Friday. You didn't care about the innocent lives you were going to take in the process, and probably still don't care. And that's exactly why I'm trying to get you to open your eyes. Some people have walked away from the street life, but there are still some that are out here doing the same sinful acts. I'm not saying that it was premeditated that you killed that innocent little girl while she was asleep in her bed. But your actions proved just how ruthless sin is! Sin will make you think you're out to do one thing, when in fact; it's blindly using you to do something treacherous. Some may argue that is not premeditated sin. However, premeditated murder is when you kill somebody and planned it in advance. So, it's premeditated sin as well, because *"thou shalt not kill"* (sin) is one of the commandments. So to go against what God has told us not to do is sin! Simply stated, disobedience is sin. Now think about this; I could've died in any given situation when I was operating in my sins! And that alone is something to be thankful for, to say the least! Somebody might ask why should I be thankful? Because he opened your eyes even when they were temporarily shut. Whenever God pulls the scales off your eyes be thankful! The fact that he opened my eyes today is a blessing within itself! Thank you Jesus for loving me, in spite of me being me! Again the subject of sin is more for "Why Am I So Comfortable Living In My Sins."

There have been times in our lives that God has given us options. He places people in our lives, sometimes only for a day. Those people are like our donkeys intended to turn us in another direction and opened our eyes. If for nothing but a quick moment, only to see the future outcomes of our bad idea, those people are important to our destiny. Those moments may have saved us not only from our own bad choices, but also from death. Like this one scripture about a talking donkey saved his master from the death angel that was standing in the road. So through this journey of *Both Eyes Open and Both Eyes Shut*, consider me your donkey that God gives the ability to see the death angel in the middle of the road. Did I mention that God opened the donkey's mouth and he began to speak to his master as well? Okay let's go a little farther then.

"That night God came to Balaam and said, since these three men have come to summon you, go with them, but do only what I tell you" (Numbers 22:20).

Before I continue, I just want to say that although many of us are unlike Balaam, we must still ask ourselves one question. "Do I have my ears open to even hear the voice of

God?" How many of us are prepared to hear that still small voice? What distractions are you willing to let go in order to hear the voice of God? Many of us are not willing to give up the things we love, because we are not sure if God will speak to us anyway. Now the difference is Balaam's ears were opened to hear. He merely disregarded what was said. How many of us have disregarded what has been spoken to us? Even when we hear the directions clearly, we still sometimes ignore God. On the other hand, some of us haven't heard anything. I would rather be able to hear the Lord and come up short trying to follow the instructions, than not to hear Him speak at all. That is the position that many of us are in today; we don't know when God is speaking to us because we are too busy with the cares of this life, and not listening. Sometimes we are listening, but to the wrong people! For example, the secular music of today consumes us to the point that reading the Word of God and cutting off the radio is a no go. People say, "I don't have time to read the Word of God and actually I don't understand it. So what is the purpose? I got to listen to my music." And why is that music becomes a part of us and we can't function without it! Sometimes God sends his Word through people. Unfortunately, we often reject the person and the message because we are expecting a bigger delivery. We often look for a bishop or somebody else with a distinguished title to come. We're looking for a message from up high, because we think to highly of ourselves than we ought to! We think we are all that, and we love those who call themselves elite or superstars. We think of ourselves as elite in our minds, because we have been deceived. In another life, we feel like we should be on a higher level than we are, so we associate ourselves with people. We live in denial of reality. As a result, we are clueless of who we are in Christ Jesus. We don't understand our own lives, because we don't understand our purpose. One of the reasons is because we have taken on the shadow of someone else. Duplicating others is never our purpose in Christ. Sometimes we get so high on our horse that we feel that God has to send us a special message from a special person. We brainwash ourselves into thinking that we are doing something special for Him! When actually we should just be glad and grateful to hear from God at all! I'm seriously encouraging people to start listening when others are trying to reason with you. It could be the message that saves your life! Even if the message comes from someone that doesn't have two nickels to rub together, still listen. *"Be careful how you entertain strangers, because they may have entertained angels unaware."* And you never know, the person you rejected might just be that donkey that God used you in that hour. *"Do not forget to show hospitality to strangers, for by so doing some people have shown hospitality to angels without knowing it"* (Hebrews 13:2).

"Balaam got up in the morning, saddled his donkey and went with the prince of Moab. But God was very angry when he went, and the angel of the Lord stood in the road to oppose him, Balaam was riding on his donkey, and his two servants were with him. When the donkey saw the angel of the Lord standing in the road with a drawn sword in his hand, she turned off the road into the field. Balaam beat her to get her back on the road. Then the angel of the Lord stood in a narrow path between two vineyards, with walls on both sides. When the donkey saw the angel of the Lord, she pressed close to the wall crushing Balaam's foot against it. So he beat her again. Then the angel of the Lord moved on ahead and stood in a narrow place where there was no room to turn, either to the right or the left. When the donkey saw the angel of the

Lord, she laid down under Balaam, and he was angry and beat her with his staff. Then the Lord opened the donkey's mouth, and she said to Balaam, "what have I done to you to make you beat me these 3 times." Balaam's answered the donkey. "You have made a fool of me! If I had a sword in my hand, I will kill you right now. The donkey said to Balaam am I not your own donkey, which you have always ridden to this day? Have I been in the habit of doing this to you! No, he said. Then the Lord opened Balaam's eyes, and he saw the angel of the Lord standing in the road with his sword drawn. So he bowed low and facedown. The angel of the Lord asked him, "Why have you beaten your donkey these 3 times? I have come here to oppose you because your path is a reckless one before me. The donkey saw me and turned away, from me 3 times, if she had not turned away, I would certainly have killed you by now, but I would have spared her. Balaam said to the angel of the Lord, I have sinned; I did not realize you were standing in the road to oppose me. Now you are displeased I will go back. The angel of the Lord said to Balaam, "go with the men, but speak only what I tell you" (Numbers 22:21-35).

Summary of Number 22:21-35

First, remember that God is all about 2nd chances; so, don't get down on yourself because you have made mistakes. Now let's go back and look at verse 22, *"but God was very angry when he went and the angel of the Lord stood in the road to oppose him."*

We have to start being aware of places we are going in life. The things that we indulge in that maybe shouldn't be taking place have the ability to affect us. In this day and age, where people don't live by the Word of God, they try to change or redefine the Bible to make it mean whatever conveniences their lifestyles. As a result, Christian churches can be confusing with all sorts of different doctrines. But

God's Word has never changed, from beginning to end. With so many different doctrines going forth, if a person doesn't truly know the voice of God, they will be lost. I don't care where you are in life right now, whether you believe in God or not, if He calls you there is nothing you can do to resist. God is All Powerful, he can do all things, and that includes calling you out of your sins! To oppose means: To go against or fight hard to stop it. God is telling us in this hour, because of our lack of faith, belief, and trust in him, angels are sent to oppose us. Considering our doubtful way of thinking and living, we can't even see the angel in the middle of the road. Despite the fact that the angel's sword is drawn, ready to take our lives, we remain blindsided.

Consider Romans chapter 13, and afterward, don't hate me, remember, I'm just the donkey. *"Besides this you know what (a critical) hour this is, how it is time now for you to awake up out of your sleep (rouse to reality). For salvation (final deliverance) is nearer to us now than when we first believed (adhered to, trusted in, and relied on Christ, the messiah). The night is far-gone and the day is almost here. Let us then drop (fling away) the works and deeds of darkness and put on the (full) armor of light. Let us live and conduct ourselves honorably and becomingly as in the (open light of) day, not in reveling (carousing) and drunkenness, not in immorality and debauchery (sensuality and licentiousness), not in quarreling and jealousy. (But clothe yourself with the Lord Jesus Christ (the messiah), and make no provision for (indulging) the flesh (put a stop to thinking about the evil cravings of your physical nature) to (gratify its) desires (lusts)"* (Romans 13:11-14).

The bottom line is that *the sin nature* has taken control of most of us. Sin has become fully-grown within our lives. We can't understand how and why we do some of the dumb things that we do, but at the time we don't consider it dumb. It's not until we have to face the consequences of our dumb actions that we understand the damage of what we did. One of the problems is that we can't disconnect the thoughts of just living life for God and living life in sin. And for this reason, God is standing opposite of us. We have to understand that a Holy God awakens us every day. And from the start of the day, unholy people fail to accredit anything to God's goodness. Yet, He loves us. Regardless of what we did yesterday, Jesus already paid the price for our sins with His own blood. God wants us to be like Himself and His son. He wants us to guided by His Spirit. He wants us be a holy people that are living acceptable lives unto Him. It gets to a point where He's faithful to us, but each and every day we are unfaithful to Him. It's no wonder why the angel of the Lord is on the same road in opposition of us! I thank God because now that I look back over my life, mercy and grace surrounds me. Every time I went to the club, and made bad decision after the next, it was by his mercy and grace. It is by his mercy and grace that I'm still alive today.

There is only one who comes to kill steal and destroy, and that is the devil. So don't get me wrong, I'm not saying God wants to send his angels out to kill you. Some people may say they got set up in certain situations, but whatever the case may be, thank God! It could've been me that got killed at a young age. Come on now, I know the life that I lived and you know the life that you have lived past, present and how you are living now will lead you into your future. For most of my adult life I know I was in some places and done some things that required mercy and grace.

The blood of the lamb, which is the blood of Christ, is the only way God sees you. God is not like us regardless of what some of you may think. While you're walking around thinking that he sees you the same way others see you, that's not a reality. I wouldn't be here today if it wasn't for the blood. I've had a gun put up too my head. I've also been chased out of neighborhoods by people we call killers – and they had every intention of doing the same to me. It was only because the blood.

I've been in some bad places, smoked-out houses, guns on the table, and alcohol everywhere. I've never carried a gun. While I was far from being a square or nerd, it seemed that the people who carried guns made themselves subject to unnecessary violence. That extra protection makes you tougher than you really are, and it can have you facing unexpected and unwanted consequences. I grew up in Gary, Indiana, and I know that the blood covered me. And did I mention, I have a praying mother, and I know that prayer works. I have been in neighborhoods that I wasn't supposed to hang out in, but God spared me.

I'm not saying that I see everything perfectly now, but I can say that I see my life in Christ clearer today. Now there are some things that still have my vision blurry, but I can say that I don't see things the way I used to see them, and that goes for the way I see people as well. I thank God for getting me off of that road of destruction. I try my best to stay off of that road that leads man to nowhere! Now some may ask, "How is it possible for one to stay off that road?" Stop doing the things that are in opposition to God. Start living right, seeking the face of God, loving one the other, praying, being thankful, and stop judging! These are of some of the ways that you can stay off of that road! Look I'm not saying that I avoid all these roadblocks everyday – I'm not saying that at all. In life, there are some roadblocks you can start avoiding, and there are still times that we might be on the wrong road and not even know it. Once I realize that I have veered off course, I pray and I try to get back in line. Sometimes we can get so far out of line, and when that happens we have to pray, pray, and pray some more. Nobody is perfect. But I do know that there are times that I might do something that puts me in jeopardy of being on the wrong road. That's when that angel just may be standing on the opposite side of me. Many others, myself included, have to decide if we want to continue to live on this road that can take our lives at any time. The wrong road is the one that puts us in jeopardy of being separated from God permanently. Staying on the narrow path requires us to change the way we think about our lives, families, friends, associates, co-workers, and even our pastors. What do I want my legacy to be? Was I one that couldn't put away the weed, the alcohol, and women? I couldn't just love my wife and children; I thought I needed other things in life to keep me happy. I didn't know how to love. I didn't know how to be committed. I didn't know how to pray. I didn't know that I had to have self-control. I didn't know how to forgive. I didn't want to give my life to Christ. I loved to party, gamble, and going to clubs. I loved having multiple women at one time. I loved living this life that the enemy wanted me to keep living. This was a life of brokenness. One day God spoke to me and he told me to go through the maze and come and find my place in him. I went through the maze, and came to a place where I saw all the things I craved. I realized my life was about money, weed, women, cars, houses, lusting, backbiting, jealousy, and my path to the top. I've seen rap music and entertainment artists in their truest forms. I've seen drug dealing and houses like the playboy mansion – I felt like I'd seen it all. And the Lord spoke to me and he told me that I made the wrong turn. He instructed me to "go back." When I went back, I was instructed to mark the place where I made the wrong turn. This way, next time when I'm navigating through life's maze, I'll go in the right direction. Then and only then, will I be able to live the purpose driven life. So, I began to walk back and do as the Lord told me. When I looked back I changed my mind. I will be able to live my purpose driven life. I wanted to live the life that I had become accustomed too when I made the wrong turn. There were so many people there that I wanted to rub elbows with. These were famous people. I figured if they made the wrong turn and they're living well, I can, too. And then he spoke to me again and told me this:

"For the ransom of a life is too costly, and (the price one can pay) can never suffice- (9) so that he should live on forever and never see the pit (the grave) and corruption. (10) For he sees that even wise men die, the self-confident fool and the stupid alike perish and leave their wealth to others. (11) Their inward thought is that their houses will continue forever, and their dwelling places to all generations; they call their lands, their own (apart from God) and after their own names. (12) People, despite their wealth, do not endure; they are like the beasts that

perish. (13) This is the fate of those who are foolishly confident, and trust in themselves, and of their followers, who approve their saying. Selah (pause for a second and calmly think about what was just said here)! (14) Like sheep they are appointed for Sheol (the place of the dead); death shall be their shepherd. And the upright shall have dominion over them in the morning; and their form and beauty shall be consumed, for Sheol shall be their dwelling. Their forms will decay in the grave, far from their princely mansions. (15) But God will redeem me from the power of Sheol (the place of the dead); for he will receive me. Selah (pause for a second again and calmly think about what is being said here)! (16) Be not afraid when (an ungodly) one is made rich, when the wealth and glory of his house are increased; (17) for when he dies he will carry nothing away; his glory will not descend after him. (18) Though while he lives he counts himself happy and prosperous, and though a man gets praise when he does well (for himself), (19) he will go to the generation of his fathers, who will nevermore see the light. (20) A man who is held in honor and understands not is like the beasts that perish" (Psalms 49:8).

Focus on verse (13), this is the fate of those who trust in themselves. This verse applies to a number of rappers and a number of entertainers. Sadly, we tend to put them above everything and everyone. Many people will even fight so-called friends if someone disrespects their favorite entertainers. The world has called them superstars and so you call them superstars. The world worships them so they call themselves gods. You will listen to Jesus walks with me; but you won't read about when Jesus walked on water! So don't tell me you haven't placed these entertainers as your gods. Three 6 mafia "f-in wit dis click" the lyrics - *"(I'm on a cross Lucifer please cut me free (cut me free) I'll draw your portrait if you pull these nails out of my feet (nails out of my feet) my cross upside down." "No Lord could stop us now cause the demons reborn again follow me into the trees watch me rob Adam and watch me rape eve."* Tech n9ne chorus demons, *"There's a demon inside of me, can I kill it? Hell no! Can I kill it? Hell no! Can I kill it? Hell no!"* Reverse the song and you can hear another message, *"Hell is coming, onward! Hell is coming, onward! Hell is going to keep us enemies my friend."* These are the people that we support. Many would say, "Their music doesn't make them bad people. That's just how they are making money. Why are you hating?"

Stop allowing these demonic spirits in your life, home, and in your marriage. Stand up for something, instead of all this foolishness that is taking place in the world today! Volume III will expose a lot of these types of behaviors, songs and artists that we adore. They will get exposed for who they really are, because they are not people of God. This stuff on television nowadays is really going against God and his will. They are gaining exposure on television and Facebook and all these other social media sites as distractions. We can be on these sites for hours at a time, but can't spend 5-minutes reading the Bible. This type of behavior has become so natural that we seldom realize it!

We tend to overlook things that superstars do. Are you able to see how highly we exalt these entertainers and athletes? We place them on pedestals. We'll spend money to go to a football or basketball game, buy Jordan's latest shoes, but we can't give our tithes. The sins of entertainers and athletes are the same as anyone else's, according to the Bible. I know I touched some people with that one, but I'm not living for you, I'm living for God. It is on my heart to tell the truth!

"Come on Cory J., you shouldn't say nothing about famous people, you just hating because you don't have the type of money and fame they do. You want to make us believe that if we follow people whom we have come to love we will go to hell. Why are you putting this in our heads and making us think about stuff like this." I didn't write the Bible. *"Don't be afraid of those who want to kill your body; they cannot touch your soul. Fear only God, who can destroy both soul and body in hell"* (Matthew 10:28). Don't hate on me because I've decided to accept God as the head of my life. Don't be mad at me because I choose to serve the true and living God.

I don't have a problem with their multi-million dollar mansions. That's cool, they are making millions on top of millions and how much are you making to support their nonsense messages? I don't know about you, but I don't want to support someone I know I don't believe in! I just can't do it! I'm not a person that is in awe of someone's super stardom. And I believe God has the same standards for us all. Don't take that the wrong way, because sure, I like celebrities like anybody else. I'm a Laker fan and have been one since 1980. I like watching Magic, Kobe, Shaq and so forth. I'm also a Cowboys fan, and have been one since the early 80's. I like Tony Dorsett, Tony Hill, Michael Irving, Emmitt Smith, and Troy Aikman. I like Denzel Washington, Halle Berry, used to love Stacy Dash, key word used too! I even love me some Toni Braxton. So I'm not trying act like I'm so far above everybody else, because I'm not. I don't feel that way at all. I'm saying that I can separate myself from other people's fame. I try to maintain an honorable standard of living based on the Bible – it's called holiness! The question is, Can you and do you? I am a fan, but I don't live my life based on what or how an entertainer or athletes thinks. I feel like what Charles Barkley said was true! All athletes are not role models. But I know a couple that are and they are my cousins, one plays for the Indiana Pacers and another one plays football for the Purdue Boilermakers.

We look to them as role models and most of them don't want us to look at them like that. Honestly, how many of them contribute to their communities or to your community? Just because somebody starts wearing skinny jeans, am I supposed to start wearing them? If somebody starts wearing high heels am I supposed to start wearing them as well? Am I supposed to start wearing skinny suits because that is what everyone else is doing, and they make it look cool? Am I supposed to wear my pants down to my ankles because other guys are doing it? It actually looks stupid on them to me, so why would I do that? Some so-called superstars wear the same clothes that their wife wear, am I supposed to wear my wife clothes as well? I don't think so – that's not happening here! I don't know these so called trendsetters, and they don't know me. Sadly, we tend to think that because we see somebody on TV, or in a few movies, or on a basketball court or a football field, or see people on stage or on some award shows we have some connection with them. We feel like we know them, "That's my boy right there," or "That's my girl right there!" You don't know these people, just like they don't know you! But if you let some people tell it, you would think that they hang out with these people on a daily basis. First off, they don't even associate themselves with individuals that are not on the same level with them. So, that means that they don't hang out with people like you and I. So, stop letting them lead you astray! I can envision somebody saying, "They are not leading me astray, I live my own life, and my life is good. Nothing about music or popular people define my life! Who does he think he's talking to?" People who are clueless about the power of influence are the main ones that are led astray.

"Then the angel of the Lord moved on ahead and stood in a narrow place where there was no more room to turn, either to the right or the left" (Numbers 22:26). My people, I'm here to tell you that a lot of us have run out of room. There is nowhere else for us to turn. We can't go to the right or the left. Either we're going to accept the plans He has for us, or we're going to choose to lose the life he gave us. It's as simple as that, it's like they used to say in the old days, "You at the end of the road!" *"When the donkey saw the angel"* (Numbers 22:27). Notice that the donkey saw the angel. See, sometimes it's that person that you think is not smart, that's corny, or the one that is not considered all that cool. Perhaps it's the person who you don't even like. Usually the one that you don't suspect, they are the ones whom God gives the vision to see what is in the road. They are not just protecting you or seeing for you alone, they are also supporting everyone that's in your circle. They see things that pertain to your future. They see your children and your children's children. In so many words, we need to stop talking about people or judging people that God has placed in our lives for that season to be our seer.

"Then the Lord opened the donkey's mouth and she said to Balaam (Numbers 22:27). Think about that, God opened the

donkey's mouth to talk. An animal opened his/her mouth and began to have a full fledge conservation with a man. The donkey had the wisdom and the understanding to not only talk but to relate back to her owner Balaam. Now, me personally, when I read this for about the 10th time, I was amazed by the power of God. The fact that God has the power to make an ass speak with logic and understanding is astounding. He gave the donkey the ability to see when everyone else around couldn't! Sometimes you need some donkeys in your inner-circle. Donkeys are those that tell you what they see, and not accept your lame response. People need to hear the truth, and that is exactly what a donkey does.

Let's finish up with *"Your path is reckless before me"* (Numbers 22:32). We better get our act together. Get it together quick, fast and in a hurry! The path that most of us are going on is a reckless one in the sight of God. An angel is in the middle of the road waiting to oppose us, because God is not happy with our direction in life. One of our reckless paths in life is talking about those whom God has anointed. People always talk about the pastors, and how all they want is the churchgoer's money. They say, "All they want to do is drive around in Cadillac's. The preacher is a man just like me trying to get to heaven. They all cheat on their wives. The people jump around and carry on like they're crazy. It doesn't take all that. Black people out here dying every day at the hands of white men, and Blacks around here praying to a white man's God. Black churches taking their money to white banks that's funding corruption against blacks. And they want me to go to church for what? I live by the street code, I'm doing my best 50 cent impersonation, *'Get Rich or*

Die Tyrin!'" Do you worry about what the weed man does with your money? For real, do you worry about what the weed man does with you money. Do you worry about what these gas station owners do with your money? When you are in there buying blunt papers, do you worry about what Tom Ford does with your money? Do you worry about what these stores in the malls do with your money? Do you worry about what these video game makers do with your money? Do you worry about what the casino owners do with your money? I used different examples because I really want to get you thinking. No, you don't worry about what they do with your money, because you are getting what you want. Even if it is killing you slowly, you don't care what they are doing with your money as long as you think you are looking good. Seriously, you don't worry about what they do with your money, but you worry about what the pastor does. It's not the pastor's money; this is what God has requested from us. God gives us the money to do the things that we enjoy. He also gives us the money to buy the things that we need. Even still, we don't trust God, or the people he has put in place to watch over our souls. However, we trust the drug dealer. Yeah, we trust the drug dealer. How many times have you been to the weed house this week? How many times have you been to church this month? Better yet, how many times have you given God thanks this year? I bet it's no more than you in been to the weed house. We even trust the liquor store with our souls. People will go to the liquor store 2-3 times a week or more, chasing a feeling. Yet, we don't go to church to get what we need, and to chase after Jesus Christ.

We trust the casino, instead of trusting God's Word. This kind of reckless thinking and reckless behavior has led us down this reckless path. "I don't want to go to church and give them my money, because they are thieves! I don't want to help the pastor obtain wealth. Who cares if he is trying to get me saved, and live my life acceptable to God? I don't care about none of that, because if the pastor is really worried about my soul then him watching over my soul shouldn't come with a price, that is what he is supposed to do right?" On the other hand, we will buy expensive concert tickets to see live entertainers, superstars, and comedians. You think they are there to entertain you, if so you're missing the real message they are sending. I will talk more about this in Volume III "Win, Lose, No Draw," spiritual warfare.

Sometimes you got to listen to that donkey. See the problem with our youth today is they really don't have any donkeys rolling with them nowadays. They all want to be chiefs. They used to say, "To many chiefs and not enough Indians." They are all leaders. A bunch of individuals who believe they know everything. Today's youth is comprised of group of lost individuals that don't know what awaits them in life. They don't want your help or your advice. "You're too old, you're out of touch, and you don't know what life is about." So, they don't want to listen to a "Has-been" or a "Used-to-be." We got children, young adults, our youth walking around as if they don't need instructions from their parents, teachers, pastors and the likes. The only ones they want to listen to be those that agree with everything they say. They want to listen to those that don't go against their plans.

They don't challenge each other, and they don't want to have any conflict. They just want to follow one another off the road into the ditch. The blind cannot lead the blind. As Sarah Palin said, "They want to follow each other off the bridge to nowhere - the blind leading the blind." *Let them alone and disregards them; they are blind guides and teachers. And if a blind man leads a blind man, both will fall into a ditch"* (Matthew 15:14). Man, in my hometown city of Gary, Indiana, in 2015, men were getting killed in double homicides! Little girls were victims of homicide. We got young men out there killing without a cause. We have to protect ourselves. When I say "protect ourselves," I mean protecting ourselves with the Word of God. For starters, every time I go into the gas station men and women alike, not just teenagers, are buying blunt papers. The gas stations don't have notebooks. They don't sell ink pens or pencils. They do have sex pills and everything else you need to sell and misuse drugs – I'm just saying! In urban communities you have a liquor store on every corner. Drugs are illegal, but they still making lots of money off of it. And now marijuana is actually legal in some states. Does that really mean the misuse of drugs is okay with God? I guess it depends on whom you ask. Now this is my thing; the same people that we claim are holding us back are the same people that are passing these laws. They are the same ones that are killing our young black men in the streets. They are the same ones that won't allow you to get a car or house loan. They are the same ones that don't want your children to go to the same school as theirs. They are upping the price on college tuition. Now if they are using corporate strategies to stunt the advancement of Black people in all this aspects of life, making drugs legal will be no different. Passing these new laws will hold Blacks back permanently. It's not just the youth that don't have donkeys in their inner circles; a lot of grown folks don't have any either. Because a lot of us think that we have everything all figured out just like the youth think they do.

Chapter 2

MY BROTHERS, MY BROTHERS, MY BROTHERS

"You are the light of the world. A city on a hill cannot be hidden" (Matthews 5:14).

"This is the message we have heard from him and declare to you: God is light; in him there is no darkness at all. (6) If we claim to have fellowship with him yet walk in darkness, we lie and do not live by the truth" (John 1 5:6).

"Anyone who claims to be in the light- but hates his brother is still in the darkness" (John 2:9).

My brothers, my brothers, my brothers: *[To my old school brothers, my young brothers, my Christian brothers, my professional brothers, my in-between brothers, my dope fiend brothers, my drug dealing brothers, to my want-to-try-the-other-side brothers, my real brothers, my pimping brothers, my street brothers, my thug life brothers, my ghetto brothers, my really-I-don't-care brothers, my professional ball player brothers, my rap and the music industry brothers, my dead beat dad brothers, my taking-care-of-my-kids brothers, my movie industry and comedian brothers, my whose keeping God first brothers, and my murdering and kill to live brothers].*

It doesn't matter what label you've been given you are still my brother. Somewhere in these shut-eyes of ours we're missing something! I just want to make it clear that some of you see clearly, and we are proud of your examples. I know there are a lot of guys who are out there that really got their entire life in total focus. All men can live a great life as long as the Lord wakes us up and opens our eyes. *"But seek ye first the kingdom of God, and all his righteousness; and all these things shall be added unto you"* (Matthew 6:33).

If my brothers would just take a look at their lives and see where they are, they might realize the importance of seeking the Lord. If we are seeking the Lord then soon we will realize that we are in the right place. And that right place is being before God, humble, giving thanks, and loving one another. But a lot of us don't seek and we have no desire to seek; so with that being said, let's dialog for a minute.

Men, yes men walking around with the maturity level of little boys! And one reason is because we don't know the difference between being a man vs. growing up and becoming a well-rounded man. God said, *"Let us make man in our image"* (Genesis 1:26-27).

We were created in the likeness of God, built with the image of God and His Son. We weren't made as God or like God, nor the Son. Unfortunately, some people want to make us believe we are equal to God. But we were made in the image of the father and the son. Men, do we really know, as a whole, our identity in the body of Christ? Have you made this personal? Have you ever just sat down and thought about your life in a righteous way? And if you have never thought about your life in a righteous way, then why do you think living a life for Christ is beneath you? Honestly today we're living in a society where men think that they are gods and some women think that they are goddesses, and that's not a joke. There is a war going on around us, and we're looking towards the Middle East, but it is in our lives every day. You don't know it, but it starts with *Both Eyes Open and Both Eyes Shut* and then it goes to why are my eyes shut? I have both eyes open and both eyes shut, because I'm comfortable living in my sins. I have to understand that in my life it's either win, lose and no draw when it come to spiritual warfare. Most people have their eyes shut, because they love living in sin. We find ourselves in bad situations because we don't know we're in a spiritual warfare.

As it relates to thinking we're gods, it's like we tend to think of ourselves just like some of these entertainers think. The thing is we have put man so far up on a pedestal that we can't tell the different between men who consider themselves as god, from the true and living God who gives us life.

"And when the people saw what Paul had done, they lifted up their voices, saying in the speech of Lycaonia, and the gods are come down to us in the likeness of men" (Acts 14:11).

This is the way they viewed men as gods, and the way people now view men, as gods are different concepts. They based their thoughts that gods have come before them in the likeness of a man of God. Oftentimes, we view men as gods because of popularity. Now we worship those who can't or won't do anything for us. We worship those who are doing things for their own selfish gain. We even worship people who don't even know us. That's another distinct difference between them and God, because God knows you. God loves you. God wants you to succeed in life. Can you say that about your favorite superstar? Do you think that they care if you succeed in life or not? I'll wait for an answer! Now if this is the case and we are putting everything and everyone else above the true and living God, we are missing the entire picture of what life is all about! Sad thing about putting man before God is people will defend man's honor to the fullest, but won't wake up and say "thank you" to God.

"Thou shalt not bow down thyself to them, nor serve them: for I the Lord thy God am a jealous God, visiting the iniquity of the fathers upon the children unto the third and fourth generation of them that hate me" (Exodus 20:5).

"For thou shalt worship no other God: for the Lord, whose name is jealous, is a jealous God" (Exodus 34:14).

"They have moved me to jealousy with that which is not God; they have provoked me to anger with their vanities: and I will move them to jealousy with those which are not a people; I will provoke them to anger with a foolish nation" (Deuteronomy 32:21).

Now these are not my words, this is the Word of the Lord. So, my brothers, why are we continuing to put this type of pressure on our families, unborn seeds, and ourselves.

The word said to the third and fourth generations. We are talking about descendants that we might not even see. Yet, they will be forever linked to you because you are the seed bearer. Therefore, why are we living careless lives knowing that we will affect future generations? As you all know, man's time on earth is short? We are just passing through before we go back home to the father and the son. No man lives forever. Which will be another subject matter presented by Moneyway. What does forever mean to you?

Pessimistic views of God, religious leaders, and church lead to misguided brothers. At some point in our lives we have to take a stand against the enemy who only comes to steal, kill and destroy. He is stealing the joy that God has given to all men through the blood that he shed on Calvary. If God is for me, then who can be against me? We are missing this brothers because many of us think that God is not with us. O'Dawg said in *Menace to Society*; "I don't think God is really with us, look at how we living. Things are all messed up!" You know brothers we listening to things in the movies or a song, and that becomes a part of our DNA. We can't separate the two, but they are two different things; movies and music are both influential forms of entertainment. But our lives have a greater destiny than that which comes from secular influences. And we should not let entertainment form our destiny in Christ Jesus.

Listening to the voice of God is important to me, that's why I limit the music I allow in my life. How can I listen to God when I have my mind preoccupied with everything else that is happening? Yes, I grew up listening to rap music, R&B and all that other stuff. But where has it gotten me, and where has it gotten you for that matter? I'm at a point in my life where music doesn't define who I am; I don't have to listen to a song to pick me up nowadays. The enemy is no longer going to steal my joy, the enemy is no longer going to kill my dreams and the enemy is no longer going to destroy my household. If I am the head of my household, I have a responsibility to be the head. The head gets his instructions from God not from a rap song. My brothers, we have to stop looking for truths in ungodly places, like *Get Rich or Die Tryin,'* is not something from God. Go back and read the scripture: *"Seek ye first the kingdom of God and all these things will be added to you."* At an early age, we learned that [a thing] is a person, place or object. So he is telling us if we seek him first: the car, house, good woman (wife), job, and money will be added.

You don't have to risk killing yourself to become rich, for the Lord said, *"I have come to give you life and give you life more abundantly.*" Honestly, did fifty die trying to get rich? No, he didn't! But he put that thought in the minds of young men. Now guys are running around talking I'm going to *Get Rich or Die Tryin,'* and are actually on the streets killing, dying, and trying to get rich. My brothers, that's a lie from the pits of hell. Seek, and God will supply all your needs, not just some of them.

"The Lord God formed the man from the dust of the ground and breathed of life and the man became a living being" (Genesis 2:7). Stop right here: He made "man." Adam was created as a man. It says nothing about him ever being a boy or a child. So my brothers when one become a certain age, it's time to become a man and put away childish things. *"When I was a child, I talked like a child; I thought like a child, I reasoned like a child. When I became a man, I put childish ways behind me"* (I Corinthians 13:11). Look brothers let's keep it real, having a wife, a sidekick and a couple of other pieces on the side is not cool. Perhaps during our younger years it may seem fun. I know this from experience, because I lived that lifestyle for a long of time, although I wasn't married at the time. It's difficult to tell young people how wrong that lifestyle is, especially when they're living it. To those of us that used to live like that, we were always trying to impress. We were still living by the enemies plan, not knowing that our *player* ways were destroying lives! One might ask, "What lives are we destroying?" First and foremost you're destroying your own life! We are also destroying the women who we are dealing with, and if there are kids involved, we are destroying their lives as well. A person might even ask, "How is it destroying the children, they are not the ones in a relationship? What we fail to realize is that it affects them more than anything. A little girl is saying to herself, "Every time I visit my daddy he has another

woman over his house." A little boy saying to himself, "Every time I look around Momma got another man in her bed saying he's her friend watching television." You don't think that in the long run that this doesn't play a part in their makeup of life? You don't think that they are keeping these images of Momma and Daddy in their heads? You don't think that they are saying to themselves, if it was good for Momma and Daddy, then it should be good for me as well? Just think about that, my brother! Think about this too, if you have two women, and the children know about both women, it will affect them. When they're older these issues will resurface. There will already be trust issues, because of their experiences. These things can follow them for the rest of their lives, and it has followed many of us. That is why some people have social issues. Come on brother, if you're beating on a child's mother in front of that child, you don't think that he might grow up and become physically abusive? Also, God forbid the battered woman tells her adolescent daughter "It's ok, your daddy (or Joe Blow) is a good man.

So many women get beat for telling men to grow up and stop being boys. The truth hurts, and triggers abuse in a lot of people, especially immature dysfunction boys who don't like to be told to grow up and handle your responsibilities. So what do you think women? It's sad, because truth is, so any of your daughters will grow up seeing what you tolerated and set their bar based on your lifestyle. "I'm the wife (or the main girl), and I know he loves me, so it'll be ok," is what you are teaching your daughters. Stop believing that lie!

This non-sense is an endless, ruthless, vicious cycle. Open your eyes and look, that man doesn't love you like you need to be loved, if he is putting his hands on you. Leave that situation, because there is a better brother out here for you. The brother you're with knows there's a man that will treat you better. That is why he's trying to bring down your self-esteem. A man should never beat up on a woman to prove to himself or for no other reason. You can prove that you are the man by doing the things that a man is supposed to do. That is how you prove yourself to be a man.

Open your eyes, the enemy comes to steal, kill and destroy. The enemy affects third and fourth generations. If our men don't change our wicked ways, our little ones will grow up acting the same or worse. And why is that; because today we are not man enough to stand up to the curses that has been put on our families. Somebody please stand up for the cause of life because your children's future depends on it.

> *"Lord, not my children, I don't care what my great-great-grand daddy did; I don't care what my great grand daddy did; I don't care what my grand daddy did; and I don't care what my daddy did, I am here Lord! I submit myself to you, because I don't want my children to go through the same things that I have been through. I don't want my children growing up and not knowing you. I want my children to succeed in life and be all that they can be in you. And today Lord, I take a stance and I will honor you and give you the glory in Jesus name. I know that you can do all things. There may be things that are impossible for man, but nothing is impossible for God. I can't open doors for my children Lord; not the doors you can open up Lord, but I do know that you can do all things. I can't provide all the things for my children that they need Lord, but you can. I don't know what the*

future holds for them Lord, but you know. So Lord I give myself over to you for the betterment of my children."

Come on brothers, pray with me, somebody please stand up for the cause of life because you children's future depends on you stepping up. Think about this, you are the seed bearer. Your daughter is the seed holder, and what God put in you to give her is for the seed to be! So think about the other lives that are intertwined with your life, instead of just thinking about yourself, because life is bigger than you!

"There is a way, which seems right to a man, but the end thereof are the ways of death" (Proverbs 14:12). In many ways, playing these games with these women can be a deadly situation - between AIDS, HIV, and brothers killing one another. Come on man. But yeah we got men killing each other because of cheating women.

Unfortunately, as men, we can't handle the aspect of women cheating. It's a pride thing. The problem is men and women think they own one another when they are in relationships. Newsflash: We don't own people, no parts of them. People are going to do what they want to do when they want to do it.

Brothers what we need to do is grow up, we really do. That controlling spirit is running rampage within us brothers, and the funny thing about some of us men. We even try to control the sidepiece. We want to put demands on her that she can't see anybody else, despite our main girlfriend or wife. Some guys are smooth with it; they make enough money where they can afford the sidepiece rent or mortgage. They can pay her bills, which causes the controlling spirit to run even more rampant. The messed up part about most of these men is that they don't have to even have their own. They don't have their main house in order, but they're helping the sidepiece. I'm not going to even talk about spiritual houses, because if you got two or more women that house is definitely not in order.

A general weakness of most men is that we try to do too much as the same time without effectively managing our responsibilities. Only God is in more than one place at the same time. We have to get out of this controlling atmosphere, and acknowledge the fact that it exists. One of the reasons we don't realize it exists is because we don't have time for ourselves. When we have a routine, we do the same things the same way every day, and it becomes our natural way of life. We have pieces of ourselves in so many different places that we are not *whole* as men. A whole man can hold down his own; a whole man can please one woman; a whole man can come home and be a father to his kids; a whole man can get off his butt and go to work; and a whole man believes in God. You know what is really messed up; it is when we try to go from point "A" to points "B" and "C" and get caught up in the moment trying to go and see the sidepiece. When men get in trouble with the law, they call the wife or their main girl, not the sidepiece, who likely caused the trouble in the first place. Now think about it brothers, does that make any type of sense?

Come on brothers, we have to start thinking more with our big heads than our bottom heads. I'm not about to bash women, but some women just want to destroy your home. You have to understand that the enemy sends what you desire, and if it's a woman that will be your distraction. It doesn't mean that woman will really desire you passionately. Most often, modern women are thinking just like men. Let me explain… A man encounters a woman who is in a relationship, you don't really want her, but you're testing her to see how far she is willing to go. We want to see if she is going to show some form of disrespect in her relationship. Now on the other hand, some men have their own woman; but it's exciting to sleep with another man's woman. The thrill of constant conversations, being missed and thought of throughout the day is exciting. Well it's the same for women.

We tell them that we really don't want to be at home with her anymore, and it's all about the kids. We don't want papers on us; paying child support; it's cheaper to keep her. We tell them we love them more than we love our wives or main girlfriend. And at this point we are talking to them more than we are talking to the lady of the house. On the flipside, if we leave our lady, the pressures that we have been getting from the sidepiece is coming to a head. We have to make a decision because she is about to the blow the roof off the joint! She is about to confront my lady, so I'm about to lose my lady anyway. The way I look at it, I won't have a place to stay and I really want to be with the sidepiece anyways, and so we leave. When we move, the sidepiece changes, attitude is bad, her demeanor changes, and she's not putting out like she used too. She just won the game man! She took you from your woman, which was her main goal anyway, and you had nowhere to go unless you go back to your momma's house! So, we call that game over!

Now you have to go back to those early conversations that you used to have with her. Oh, and don't forget that she has guys calling the house as well. See, when we first get the girl, we come with our whole life story, some of it is funny and some of it is sad. Men say, "My father wasn't at home so that made me the man that I am; angry, confused, controlling, self-centered. You know I didn't have a man around to teach me how to become a man. You're 30-years-old now player, stop holding on to that crutch. My mother stayed in the streets and I had over 5-step-daddy's in my lifetime. Truth is they really weren't my step-daddies, they were just my mother's boyfriends, and soon as I got attached to one, he'd leave and here comes another. The story continues… *"So, I had to fend for myself and become the man of the house at an early age. So I stayed in the streets and did what I did. One day I got caught up, that's why I don't have a job now, because I got some papers on me, and the White man is making it hard out here on a brother."* See that is the same thing we told our lady at home and she fell for it, but after a while that story runs short. We have to get to a place of having no more sob stories to tell and no more pity parties – these become excuses. With excuses we have women buying us clothes, putting gas in our cars, and giving us beer and club money. We do the things that we do because we think it's cool and acceptable. In the process, we are only putting ourselves in bad situations. Most of the time there is no real love, just sexual pleasures.

Both men and women who live this lifestyle have a lying spirit. Sometimes your whole relationship can be based on a lie. See, it's easy to lie to a woman when we're lying to ourselves every day. We're lying to ourselves when we say, "I'm good," and our lives are a train wreck. We're lying when we say, "I don't need God," when He is the only reason we're alive. There is nothing that we did so good on yesterday that we deserve to see today. If you let some people tell it, they are God's gift to the world. In a sense, you are right, but not in the way you're thinking. We're lying to ourselves when we think that hurting women and leaving children behind is just the way that it is.

No, that's not the way it goes. You haven't gotten over some things that apparently happened when you were a child? I admit, I know it hurts leaving children behind, lying to myself that it will all work itself out one day. You pray and hope for positive results, but it's doesn't always work out the way you planned. It's bad and damaging telling our kids we are going to do something and never do it. Promising to pick them up and never showing up is even worse. Telling them we are going to buy them something and failing to do so sets standards that are difficult to change. And if any of you brothers have been in this type of situation, love your children, reach out, and try to talk to them. Try to get pass the pain you've caused regardless of how humiliating it might be to your pride. Kids don't really understand the things that life will throw at them. As adults, the challenges they'll face, they might be upset now, but when they are mature enough to understand life their perspectives about your mistakes will likely change. Regardless of how a woman's decision might affect a man's relationship with his children, she should not stay stuck in an unhealthy relationship. A woman does not have to put up with a cheating and lying spirit. A man shouldn't tolerate unhealthy relationships either. We have to stop thinking and acting like we're the only perfect fit for our significant other. I forgot most of us got it like that. Man, please, most of us need to grow up. Believe this brothers, your woman may love you and may wash your dirty drawers, but don't believe for one second that your behavior is not being monitored. If it doesn't change over time, that woman will find comfort in another man arms, and even his bed. You didn't want to hear that I know! See, men and women are different when it comes to cheating.

Most women are not just out here cheating just to be cheating. Well, there are always exceptions to that rule, but some women are ruthless these days. Men will cheat just for the fun of it. The excitement of talking that talk and seeing how far we can go with it causes men to do some foolish things. We think home will always be in tact, but the moment you start cheating you've already lost your darn family! I often hear women brag about cheating "better than" men. Brothers, a woman is not cheating just to be cheating; she is cheating to find your replacement – yes your replacement! Yeah she is looking for that brother who doesn't play video games all day. Women want men who will provide, pay attention, go on dates, and listen. If you know that you are not doing these things for your woman, than don't go on a killing spree because she found what you were not. Brothers, at times we get caught up in the wrong stuff; how good a woman looks, her sexy body, her house, and does she have a nice car. Cheating women will set us for a hard fall. Truth is, both men and women need to stop playing games.

Brothers we need to really start thinking about what kind of team do we want. Do we want a winning team or a losing team? Have you ever wondered why it seems as though we can't keep a winning team? The fact of the matter is, it's not the team that's losing it's the coach. In other words, it's your non-coaching self that keeps you from winning. This is life coaching not professional sports. You're coaching for eternal life, and that's a game you really don't want to lose. These are some things we need to consider in building a winning team:

- Am I building people up the right way, or just building my own kingdom and just misusing people?
- Am I listening with my ears or with my bottom head?

- Am I asking the right questions to develop right relationships, or am I going into this relationship (marriage) with cracks in my foundation?
- Are their goals compatible to mine?

Character is what makes a man. So, in that aspect of life we need to start self-examinations and start rebuilding. Brothers, we need to walk in love *"Therefore be imitators of God as dear children. And walk in love, as Christ also loved us and given himself for an offering, a sacrifice and us to God for a sweet-smelling aroma. But fornication and all uncleanness or covetousness, let it not even be named among you, as is fitting for saints; let no one deceive you with empty words, for because of these things the wrath of God comes upon the sons of disobedience"* (Ephesians 5:1-3).

We must eliminate unnecessary burdens in our lives. We must create expectations of those around us and ourselves. We need to have an understanding of one another. We have to start loving more, being more patience and open-minded, but most importantly, we need to start teaching our children better life lessons. Give them more options in life. We need to teach our children the love of God, so that they won't turn to the streets. Street love is tough love, and it's all about the love of money, which is fake love that equals no love *"There is a way that seems right to a man, but its end is the way of death"* (Proverbs 14:12). *"Apply your heart to instruction, and your ears to words of knowledge"* (Proverbs 23:12).

My brothers, we need to start loving our sisters more and stop beating and killing them. If the relationship is over, let it be over. If you have kids, just take care of your children; spend time with them show them love. Let the mother go, especially if either one of you have already walked away emotionally. So what if she was with someone else when you had her. Truth is, you didn't want her anyway. Okay, if she's beginning to find her way, give her room. If she's moving towards her personal goals in life that don't include you, let her do that. Once she finds out that you're no good for her, and she walks away, let her. You knew that she had a loving heart, but you didn't want that, so, let it go!

Pride won't let that happen without putting in our 2cents. That's why many of us are in jail, for killing ex-wives, ex-girlfriends, and sleeping partners. Listen to what I said, "sleeping partners" – That's all she was. Realize the truth now before it's too late. Brothers, this is what *"Both eyes open and both eyes shut"* is all about.

Chapter 3

THE INTERVIEWS
105.9 The Moneyway Show
(Raw and Unedited)

THE INTERVIEWS
1ST INTERVIEW WITH CHILLY MAC

C.J. Moneyway: Today, on 105.9 The Moneyway Show "G.O.D given our destiny" we have with us my man Chilly Mac; now my man used to be a player/player but now he is a deacon at true love international, but he is not here to talk about his deaconship but he is here to talk about his both eyes open and both eyes shut experiences. Now this is a topic we will have for the next couple of days, tomorrow we'll have the mother of Táchira banks and Táchira's ex-boyfriend the man who killed her, they will be on the show tomorrow and Wednesday we will have the lovely and beautiful NaNa Love on the show. Ok Moneyway listeners without further ado my man my friend Chilly mac. What's up mac?

Chilly Mach: What's up C.J.

C.J. Moneyway: Glad to have you here today to share your life story Chilly Mac.

C.J. Moneyway: Ok, Chilly tell us about some of your both eyes open and both eyes shut moments in your life. C.J. Moneyway, like at the beginning: you know some things you which you would have done better had you only knew the consequences; or things that still affects your life now some 10\15\20 years later.

Chilly Mac: I would have to say that when I was a teenager up until my mid 30's; I thought that I knew everything. Not that I'm a fan but I felt like Kanye West "You couldn't tell me nothing." And that's just how I felt at the time C.J.; I would listen to my parents about certain things, but when I made my mind up about something I was going to do what I wanted to do regardless of how anybody felt about it, it didn't matter to me.

C.J. Moneyway: So what were so of those certain things that you're speaking about Mac?

Chilly Mac: Like dealing with women first of all C.J, I love women. I always have and I always will, although I'm a one woman man right now, but I will always love women. My thing is I just wish I didn't personally try to love so many back in my hay day. For one I was putting my life in danger by being with so many women in my lifetime. And most men know that when you sleep with a female 2-3 times, you're basically in a relationship, well that is at least how it was in the 90's and early 2000's, nowadays people are just hanging out and sleeping with each other no commitments; but after that 2nd or 3rd time I wasn't using any protection. And I was doing this with many women; and I know people C.J. that has died doing some of the same things I used to do. People in died from aids from having unprotected sex, my eyes were shut to this form of living C.J., I wasn't thinking about dying at the time although what I was doing there was a high possibility of me doing just that; but by the grace of God he saved me from myself C.J., he saved me from myself, he protected me from any hurt harm or dangers, when I didn't even know I was in dangerous territory. You know C.J. the word says that the wages of sin is death. And I was committing the ultimate sin, I was committing sexual sins defiling my body, violating the temple God has given me to be made holy and acceptable to him. I was doing anything, but I was too busy enjoying what the enemy kept throwing my way; and I wasn't caring about no temple meaning I wasn't caring about my life, and if one is not caring about his or her own life, how can you care about someone else life? And I feel like a lot of our youth and not just them, this thing goes way beyond age, but I see people falling into these same type of traps today and they don't even know it.

C.J. Moneyway: I agree with you Mac, the enemy is definitely setting traps for all of mankind regardless of age. Mac we have grown folks who are still falling in these horrible pits that the enemy is setting up. For one we don't have enough parents praying for the youth; we need not only pray for our own children, but for our grandchildren, our nephews, our nieces, our cousins, our friends children, our associates children, our co-workers children; too often Mac people make prayer about themselves if they pray at all. When R. Kelly came out with that song "prayer changes" people thought it was cool to start praying if they didn't before, but after the song faded away, so did their prayers. Mac we as a whole believe that because things are going good in my life, my children are good, everything around me seems to be going well, when things are like that and we start thinking like that, we be like why do I need to pray, my life is going good, money in the bank, I'm driving a 2016 BMW, my kids are getting good grades in school, we take vacations on the regular, my job is providing what I need for me and my children, and my husband is providing for the entire family, so what can prayer do that is not already being done, that's how we think sometimes Mac. But what they don't realize is that somebody prayed for them, somebody prayed for their offspring's before their offspring's were even born, somebody prayed them into the life they are living now because God granted the prayers of the one or ones who prayed. Did you get it Mac, he granted the prayers of the person or persons who prayed for them. But if one don't believe that they were prayed in and now if they don't continue to pray, than at some point the prayers of those of old gets cut off, because now you are of age to begin praying for yourselves and your family, but if you make up your mind not to pray sometimes people start to see things changing in their lives the things that used to be is not the same it just seems like sometimes the things that was getting them by is not doing the same way it used too, that money that once was good is not as good anymore, that new car is not as new, those shopping sprees isn't happening as regular as they used too. People have to understand Mac, that the education they got it was prayed for to get them the job that was prayed for to get the house that was prayed for to have the cars to sit in front of that house was also prayed for but you feel like you've done it all on your own and now when God takes his hand out of your situation, I didn't say that he would leave because he said that he would never leave us or forsake us.

Chilly Mac: I feel you on that one C.J.; I remember when my mother used to take me to church with her every Sunday when I was younger. But when I got to the age where she left it up to me to go to church or not I choose not to go; for one I didn't understand what the preacher was talking about in the first place. And I didn't want to get up that early on Sunday's, it didn't matter that I went to school for a longer period of time and I had to get up earlier on top of that; and now that I'm grown I have to get up and go to work every day and I really don't like going there on the daily, but I do it, and in the meantime I can't and I couldn't get up to go to church on Sunday for a couple of hours. But here it is God give us 24-hours a day, 168 hours a week, 40-hours a week at work, but to spent 2-3 hours with God who awakes up every day, he who opens our eyes every morning, he who open the doors for us with the jobs with have or in had in the past and the jobs that has already been prepared for us in the future, but 2-hours is too much, can't do it!

I didn't understand it C.J. at that time, but I understand it now, when I choose not to give God the time he desired from me the things he had for me was withheld from me. You know C.J. I hear it all the time, "You can't beat God's giving!" Now when you choose not to have God as the head of your life, you are subject to all kinds of attacks on your life by the enemy. Like me soon as I got a new job a good paying job I would say; I had multiple babies on the way and they wasn't twins either, I was living that kind of life. And soon afterwards I got another call from another female I had been dealing with saying she was pregnant as well. Man, man, man! And for the next 10-years or so that was the story of my life, it was baby after baby; I couldn't get my feet on solid ground or nothing. Child support, pampers, baby milk, and C.J. I can truly say that period in my life was when I really had both eyes open and both eyes shut! I had my eyes open to all the things that the enemy wanted me to see, the things I desired and I never seen to be able to resist the enemy, because at that point and time in my life I didn't know anything about the enemy, that only comes to steal, kill and destroy! I was living my life telling these women how much I loved them and I really didn't; having sex with multiple women at the same time with no protection thinking back then that I was a player, and not realizing that all along the devil was playing me against me! He was playing my desires against my desires; my desires had me loving what I loved, but doing it out of order and out of the will of God. And 20-years later C.J., I can sit here and tell you today that I'm still dealing with my shut-eyes experiences. The only difference is I'm just dealing with them in the presence of God now in a family structure. And I thank God for allowing me too still be here and be able to handle and deal with my shut eyes experiences as I press on toward the goal to win the prize for which God has called me heavenward in Christ Jesus. How do I know that God has called me to something higher than myself, is because I choose to change the direction of my life and now I can see the difference in my life!

C.J. Moneyway: I'm glad you came by today Chilly Mac and gave us your story, because I truly believe that some young brothers and sisters out there needed to hear your story. Especially about the kids, because some people that have multiple children out of wedlock don't like talking about that part of their life. People seem to always want to judge others for their actions as if they have never done anything wrong or out of order. Like me Chilly, I have 3 children and 2 are out of wedlock and so that is 2 of my children that don't live with me; and since I've been married and have a baby with my wife I see the different in raising a child up on the inside and raising a child or children on the outside and I know that there is a difference.

But I get it now Chilly Mac, I used to be the type of guy that said no other man is going to raise my kids even if I was not with the mother at the time. And at one point in my life I was just like some of these other guys out here today, I was trying to control my household which I didn't have control over come to find out later on in life and trying to control my kids mother household as well. I was going to keep coming over to make sure nobody else was coming over spending time with my kids and not only with my kids, but with my kids mother; come on brothers, we know we are a little selfish like that and some guys think that they are going to be able to control that situation for the rest of that child's life! Good luck with that fellows and this is one of the reasons that a lot of brothers are dead or in jail, trying to control a situation that can't be controlled and trying to control people that don't need to be controlled, or should I say that can't be controlled. So to my brothers quite trying to be so controlling and women now of days you all are just as bad!

Look guys you can still be a father to your children when you're not with that woman, you don't have to be sleeping with your baby momma to be a father to your child; look if you are trying to move forward with your life and you got another woman or whatever trying to be so controlling can only be trouble in the long run it can only bring drama in your life. This is what I learned Chilly Mac; if you dog a female that you in have a baby by and later on it doesn't work out and there is no real closure, there will be some anguish towards you and it's possible it can be there for the reminder of the time you all know each other it's possible. I believe that when a woman gives herself to you in that manner where she is loving you and having sex with you without protection and has changed something's about her life to try to please you and show you that she loves you or really cares about you, there was a trust there as a man we broke and most of us don't even apologize for the wrong we have done! But that trust factor issue is she trusted you, she may have loved you in a way she haven't loved another man before; she might wanted you to marry her and may had wanted you to stick around for a while you know maybe for a lifetime. She may had wanted to be with you and raise your child together, but a lot of us men I don't believe that we really be thinking like that; I'm not saying all women are like this because all men don't think like this or have been in situations like this but there are many that are and have been and there will be many that will be in this situation later on in life or it's about to happen in the presence; and I'm saying all women feel like this either, because we are living in times where women are living just as reckless as men are and so their mind frame is not on this level either; I'm just saying! But Chilly Mac you know we can get in situations where child support is just not enough, sometimes women want blood they don't want to see you with a pot to you know what in; Chilly Mac you know I'm telling the truth! I'm not going to ask you how many children you have; but I see brothers that have or in had a lot of money put themselves in these type of situations; yeah the rich and the famous having both eyes open and both eyes shut! Look at DMX who has 9 kids. The guy owes over $1million in child support. Tell me was he seeing clearly? And then you can be like Nas having to pay his ex-wife $299k. If he could do it all over again, do you believe he would have wanted someone that was leaving milkshake all in the yard? Chad

Johnson has 4 kids, and paying $5k a month for 1 child. He's worth $15million, but money sometimes stop look at his career that's over with, but that child support doesn't stop! Then you got your boy T.O (Terrell Owens) on TV crying; don't get me wrong I've cried about that stuff before as well but not in front of millions of people Chilly Mac; your man is behind $120k a month in child support and mortgages all owed to 4 baby momma's; see Chilly we're not the only one that couldn't see our future while we were in the present back then. Man the champ Evander Holyfield he really had his eyes shut $327k in back child support and he owes one baby momma $500k in support that's $800k, but come on man. Yeah, I know Evander made something like $300million in his boxing career! 12kids I'm not judging him I wish I could say that I made over $300million in my lifetime, I just may have had 20-25 kids with the way I was living if I ever had that type of money and that is for real! I mean there are times in our lives that we just don't wrap up, we never met a piece that we didn't like, we liked the way she smelled, the way she looked that way she made me feel all that. So don't get me wrong Moneyway listeners I love my children and I will do anything for them; have I always been perfect by no means no! The thing is I can only be in one place at one time and if I'm not in the house watching my kids grow up, if I'm not seeing their every step them coming in and leaving out, I'm missing a big part of their lives. But one thing I do know Chilly Mac is that if I had my eyes open 20-years ago I would had made some better decisions in my life.

Well ladies and gentlemen that's our show for today we will like to thank our special guest Chilly Mac for coming and sharing his both eyes open & both eyes shut experiences with us today. I would like to also thank our sponsors and all my Moneyway listeners; thanks for tuning in today and I hope you will tune in tomorrow when we will have Denise Banks and company talking about the life of Táchira Banks. Until the next time this is C.J. Moneyway saying God bless you and peace.

THE INTERVIEWS
2ND INTERVIEW

C.J. Moneyway: Today, on 105.9 The Moneyway Show "G.O.D. given our destiny" today we will be talking about a young lady whom I believed had the brightest, of brightest future ahead of her only for it to be cut short by her than boyfriend Ike Brown whom I have also interviewed for this piece along with her mother Denise Banks, so without further time laps let's get into the Táchira Banks story.

November 1st 1979 to October 31st 2015

Táchira Banks a.k.a. T.T. Rest in peace

An angel was called home to be with the Lord, may she bring the Lord joy as she bought all of us!

(Philippians 3:12-14) *"Not that I have already obtained all this, or have already been made perfect, but I press on to take hold of that for which Christ Jesus took hold of me. (13) Brothers, I do not consider myself yet to have taken hold of it. But one thing I do: forgetting what is behind and pressing toward what is ahead, (14) I press on toward the goal to win the prize for which God has called me heavenward in Christ Jesus."*

C.J. Moneyway: Táchira Banks A.K.A. T.T., was a very beautiful woman whom I had the pleasure of getting to know personally about 6-years ago. Actually in 2008 she became my personal barber after meeting her at the church we both attended (True Love International) in Griffith, Indiana on Cline Avenue. T.T. She was a very easy going young lady, very approachable and helpful regardless of her growing status over the years of being owner and founder of T.T. Elite, LLC which was located in downtown Chicago; she owned a beauty salon and barbershop; and 5-years after opening her first beauty salon she opened up a barber and salon college school. The first one she opened was in chic town that was connected to her venue in Chicago; she eventually had 5 other shops and 2 other schools one in the New York area, she had another one in the L.A. area. Her other salons were located in Philly, Detroit and Atlanta and not to mention the numerous car dealerships that she owned. T.T. Had made herself a successful businesswoman over almost the 21-years she was in the hair business; the car dealerships came about through her ex-boyfriend and father, we will talk about them later on in this story. Táchira had over 1500 clients who would visit her shops regularly $60 a pop and on top of that she was also a personal hairstylist for about 150-200 celebrities $500-1000 a pop!

All the people she trained were just like her she put her stamp on everything she did which gave her the freedom to go from state to state and do her thing, and it allowed her to continue building her brand worldwide. Táchira even had hair products that are still on the market to this day she also had business venues in japan and china. Now here in the chic she had a place of business that was 3 stories tall in the downtown area which was over 20,000 square feet what a beautiful place it is;

as was the other establishments that she owned. Let's see you have T.T. Elite barbershop, along with a game room with a waiting room with 10 60"inch flat screens, yes the room was that big, stop by and see it for yourselves one day, there is 2 eateries, and a full size bar on the 1st floor not to mention a car dealership that is also on the first level with over 300 cars on the lot daily, and it was said that they sold about 200-250 cars a week; but she had the one who eventually killed her running the car dealerships. On the 2nd floor is T.T. Elite beauty shop, which included a spa, and a massage parlor there is also a coach outlet store on the floor along with a T.T. Elite Nail Shop, a champagne and wine bar, a minimized gym, and a children day care center with its own caregivers! On the 3rd floor is a barber and beauty/ cosmetology school with over 200 students that are currently enrolled in all 3 locations; at $20,000 a pop for each student rotating in and out every 6-months to a year, we talking over $6.6 million annually for the schools along which she received 80% of all aid that was provided for the students. In all over 50,000 people walked through T.T. Elite doors a month in all 5 states.

At the time of Táchira's death she was becoming a major brand that was steadily growing and growing. Táchira net worth was estimated at somewhere around $360 million, which when she died her mother received $3million with a $1million being in cash; $15million was given to true love international and another $15million went to the T.T. Banks foundation for sexually assaulted and abused women. And the rest went to her father! Now you might wonder how her mother received just $3 million dollars, and her foundation and the church received $15million each; and of all people, her father got the rest of her wealth.

Well you will soon find out how that came about but that's not forget that Táchira's life was not just based on how much she left to anyone; or how successful she had become, think about what Táchira accomplished, which as you will see as well was a great feat in her life considering all the things that she had to deal with; but let's see how Táchira amassed so much wealth in her 36-years of life. I'm going to tell you now you might not believe some the things that she had went through in her life, and some might even wonder how did she survive it all let alone become one of the richest women in the world.

C.J. Moneyway: Táchira banks was born on November 1st 1979, her mother Denise Banks was a well-known prostitute on the streets of chic town; her father who she never knew until she was around 20-years old was a big time chic town prosecutor. I asked Denise how did a prostitute and a prosecutor come together and have a baby. Seeing that they were on 2 sides of the fence.

Denise Banks: I was dealing with this one pimp and he had me running some drugs for him, and one day we were in his car and he had a kilo of cocaine in the trunk, we got pulled over and the police searched the car and found the cocaine; we both got arrested and went to jail. And this is how that man came into my life! He told me in a private room that he heard others around his office say that I was good at what I did and if I gave him what he wanted he would release me with no charges since I was just a passenger but if I didn't I could receive up to 10-years in prison; and if I was really good he would cut my pimps time as well. So BJ, CJ, and DJ whatever your name is; I gave that man the best of what this chic town street girl had to offer! I told him to use protection but he was talking about how he wanted to feel it and he did not come out when he was finished with his business and at the time either one of us though anything about I was getting released and my daddy was only going to get a few years, so I was cool with that. But a few months later I found out that I was pregnant and you talking about getting my head beat in on more than one occasion by some of my pimp daddy's; see when my main man Jack Mack was locked up I was on the streets by myself and I needed protection so I got plenty of it, but with protection comes a price which I paid for plenty of times! But when I found out that I was pregnant I knew it was that Billy Guy, because I used protection all the time, even with my pimps. So I called him after Táchira was born and threaten to expose him if he did not take a blood test and take care of this child since he was a big time prosecutor and all! Plus I needed the drug money and what I really wanted him to do was take the baby and raise her with his already made family because honestly I was in no position to raise a child; what was I going to do with a child! I was a drug addict and a high profile prostitute you know what they say on the streets; you can't turn any working girl like me into a mother!

C.J. Moneyway: So, Denise how did you start hooking in the first place, what happened in your life that turned you into selling your body for money; and after having this beautiful little girl you couldn't turn away from these types of activities?

Denise Banks: You don't know me like that A.J., you really don't; I was not always a professional server you know. Actually I had a great upbringing, by father worked at the ford plant and provided a good living for me, my mother and sisters; he wasn't never at home! But mom always said that he was a good provider. And for your information I was an honor roll student all the way from junior high school, until my junior year of high school, that's when I met Bobby Jackson the football and basketball star of Tinley High School, I was also the captain of the cheerleading team so yes I had some kind of morals and integrity at some point in my life. I went off to college I didn't do well because I fell in love with partying and doing drugs, more than reading and writing papers. College was a fun experience but I wasn't interested in school anymore; I was missing bobby who went off to UCLA and became a big star there and he entered the NBA in 1973 and forgot all about me can you believe that C.J. he forgot all about me of all people, I loved that man! So at that point I started seeking love in all the wrong places, dating all kind of men, but at that point I wasn't who I became; I was a bank teller at gainer bank back then and this guy used to come in all the time; he looked good he smelled good he dressed nice, and he used to always want to come to my window, and I was liking what I was seeing about 3 times a week; and I really liked what I saw in his bank account he kept anywhere between $250,000-$300,000 in his saving account and about $60,000 or so in his checking account. I thought he was a businessman or something, Jack Mack! And one day he asked me out on a date, and me being me I said yes, I thought I had finally found someone that would help me get over Bobby Jackson. So on the night we went out he asked me if I wanted to come and work for him and make some real money; I was only 22-years old at the time, with a pretty face, thick in the hips and tight in the waist, yet I was a 38-28-38, C.J., I was fine; yes I was! You probably can't tell by looking at me now, but I had it going on my man. So in the end I told him yeah I wanted to make some money, I knew he had money so I thought that maybe he would help me make a good living; I was so ready to leave the bank I couldn't stand my manager, she was a hater and all the rest of them girls in there as well, because they didn't have what I had, good looks a body to match and intelligence! So the next day he came and picked me up, he took me on Michigan Avenue and Ohio Street; we were sitting in the car and all of a sudden he told me to get out, and go stand on the corner and start making money; I was like what! And he pulled a gun out on me and told me to start making him some money, and don't say a word, and do whatever they want me to do; K.J., I was confused I was crying because I thought this guy wanted to be with this perfectly built woman, but he wanted to use me to make him some money; and then I started thinking that money he had in the bank, I saw then how he was getting it and I knew that there were more girls just like me, that he had doing this; so he stopped talking and waved the gun at me one more time and I got out, and immediately this car pulled up on me and asked me how much and I told him a $100, I didn't know and he took me around the corner in an alleyway and I was on the block for the next 15-years. Mack saw how easy it was for me to make him money, he took me to start charging $250 for the whole deal, of course that was after he tried me out and saw for himself how good I was at doing what I do, and within the next 3 to 5-years I was the one every john wanted to see on the block; they called me Miss Goodie Goodie; I worked all the blocks, Y.J., Mack told me on madison between Cicero and Kostner, Clark Street between Kinzie and Grand, North Avenue, West Armitage and Pulaski, 47th and 57th street, 71st and 76th street; I was all over the place, I was the one baby, if you didn't have Miss Goodie Goodie, you had a nobody. So yeah C.J. to answer your question I wasn't born this way I was made this way. I started at the age of 22, and officially didn't stop until I was around 42-43years old, and I had Táchira at the age of 27. I was still in my prime, but by this time the drugs and alcohol had started to play a major role in my life; and from the time I met Jack Mack to the day my parents died, they never spoke to me again, I wasn't allowed to come to the house and my sisters disowned me, because of my lifestyle. My father died about 10-years ago and my mother died 2-years-ago, and I did not go to either one of their funerals and to this day that ways heavy on my heart; because they did so much for me, when I was a kid, they took me to so many places and showed me so much love; at times I hate the day that I ever met Jack Mack, because from the time I met him, my life at the time I didn't know it, but my life was ruined and the love that Táchira deserved, I couldn't provide it and now she's gone as well and I have nothing left; I can blame Ike, I can blame jack, I can blame Billy but in the end I guess I have nobody to blame but myself!

C.J. Moneyway: I'm sorry to hear about your parents and the situation that you had with them Denise; and you're right you could blame a lot of people, but as it seems like you had done, what a lot of other people need to do and that is to look at themselves in the mirror, and realize that some of the errors that you have committed in life is not everyone else fault, those are situation that you put yourself in and you choose to commit those acts, nobody can make you do anything that you don't want to do, you always have choices so own up to them; thank you Denise you might help some people with your experiences on what not to do; especially when you have parents that supports and love you, with the way things are going in today's society; you have parents killing their kids nowadays, sexually abusing them and physically abusing them, selling them to the dope man for drugs, all kind of things, so to have 1 or both parents that loves you and wants to see you do good in life is a gift these days so enjoy it people or you could end up like Denise; you don't have to be a call girl to live a life like Denise, we all are thrown different obstacles in life that can lead you into a life similar to Denise and the similarities are a dark path with no way out, I know I have been there myself. Moving on, now I used to talk to Táchira quite often, and she told me about how she was sent to a couple of foster homes, back when she was about 9-years-old. It was said that her mother Denise took Táchira to a drug house and left her in the car for about 12-hours or so, with the windows rolled up on an 80-degree day. And this was the beginning of Táchira's 2nd phrase of life.

Denise Banks: I took her to a drug house but I left the windows rolled up it was nice outside the doors were locked plus it was a good neighborhood, so I don't know why everyone was tripping. I bought her some fries before we went over there. They took my baby away from me after that situation. They took my baby!

C.J. Moneyway: Ok, but Denise you should had known better than to leave a 9-year-old in a car by herself, come on Denise and because you bought her a bag of French fries that was going to make what you did ok, we hear you Denise. Anyway readers, after child protective services took Táchira she was put into her first foster home, she was put in a home with 13 other kids and the caregivers name was Miss Darling, and out of the 13 kids only 2 were her actual kids, 2 older boys. From the age of 10 until she was 13-years old, Miss Darling's 2 sons sexually assaulted Táchira; now there was another young lady who was around the same age as Táchira, who was being sexually assaulted as well. After years of this type of treatment Kalona

Wright, ran away from Miss Darling's home, and CPD as well as child protective services were contacted and Miss Darling's home was raided. Táchira was questioned by everyone, and was then taken to the hospital for further examined. Ms. Darling lost the 9 other foster children, and she and her sons were charged with 15 felony charges, all charges pertaining to dealing with minors. After all those offenses, Miss Darling didn't do any time, and the boys only did 3-years each. From then, Táchira was placed in another foster home 6months later, this time with a nice Christian couple, Mr. & Mrs. Adam McKingston. It was around this time that Táchira A.K.A. T.T. started doing hair and she began going to church with the McKingston's. So technically T.T. Started doing hair at the age of 15, she started off doing Mrs. Kingston's hair, and her clientele quickly grew and T.T. Became a neighborhood name on the Westside of Chicago. She was doing all the girls hair in the neighborhood, and then it was the girl's hair at school, and she even started cutting men hair and that clientele grew as well. With all of this going on in Táchira life, she began failing in school. So, Mr. & Mrs. Kingston tried to figure out a way to help T.T. to balance her life. They decided that Mrs. Kingston would start booking T.T.'s appointments instead of having about 10-20 people waiting at a time. And Mr. Kingston planned on remodeling their basement and in an 8-month period, the basement became T.T. Salon. In the process T.T.'s Grades started getting better, to the point that she graduated with honors some 3-years later. Along with making over $1000 a week in a 3-4year period, and from her own mouth she said that she didn't buy anything; she wasn't caught up in the materials things at that time, she just knew through her trials, she wanted to overcome and beat all odds; so she lived on the allowance that the Kingston's set for her, $50 a week. So, when

T.T. graduated, she had something like $156,000 to $200,000 in her bank account. It wasn't long after T.T. Graduated that her and her real mother started to talk again.

C.J. Moneyway: I spoke with Ike Brown who is Táchira's killer and ex-boyfriend, is currently on death row at Orange Mid Prison in Texas. I wanted to know why he did what he did and how did he come into contact with Táchira Banks in the first place.

Ike brown: Yeah you know I met T.T., she was living with my uncle and aunt. You know what I'm saying, I put that on the chic; yeah I knew T.T. way before she became this so-called famous hairstylist, way before she became this supposed-to-be model, and way before that punk that plays for the Chicago Tides. He's lucky he wasn't there; I would have killed him too, on the chic! But yeah when T.T. moved in with my peoples I used to go over there regularly first I used to let her braid my hair you feel me; I use to like the way she touched me, you know what I'm saying on the chic; then I used to let her cut my hair, she used to give some tight bald fades on my mamma; can't lie about that she was good with them clippers! You know than after a while I started hitting that, she was young she was only like 15-years-old and I was age 20, so you know I had some years and experience on her, plus I was a pimp you know what I'm saying. Hey look a here, she was already sexually active you feel me; you know being sexually assaulted and all for a couple of years. So I ran my game on her, she was getting paid, so I was getting paid to, she was making about $3k a week easily, easily! All she did was do hair, she never went outside, she didn't party, she didn't do anything but hair, and wait for me to come through, whenever I came through and did that thing you know. I was getting gas money, gym shoe money, club money, hotel money, rental car money, and 8 ball money; so I was hustling like a pimp at the time, keeping a little ends in my pocket here and there, you know my trick out money came from the 8balls; because T.T. Was keeping my pockets right with everything else I didn't have to buy anything with my own money, not on myself, my lady took care of that; and if she didn't I would beat that head in, she knew the deal; what! Yeah I popped that eye a couple of times you feel me, sometimes you just got to get them in line; I put that on the chic! Regardless of me dotting that eye and slapping that head every now and then, she should had been thanking me if you want to be honest with you; because I'm the one who got her and her crack head momma back together you know what I'm saying; yeah momma was trying to clean herself a little bit, but she was still on that stuff; and she was who she said she was on them streets to man! Trust me I know firsthand, isn't nothing like a crack head! If it wasn't for me, she probably would have never talked to her crack head momma again, you never know what you might find on these street; hookers, crack-heads, you never know, and her momma was both! You know after I got them back talking to one another, after T.T. graduated from high school, her momma started dogging a brother, forgetting about those broke nights she used to have and begging a brother for some work; you know telling T.T. To leave me alone, you know I was a street guy that was never going to change, and I was no good, and with my violent behavior I might just kill her one day, and telling her that I would never amount to nothing; can you believe that! We talking about a crack head and a hooker, talking about I would never amount to nothing, so I had to start going upside T.T. Head even more because she started talking crazy to a brother, listening to all that nonsense her crack head momma was talking about. Her momma must had wanted a brother or something, all to herself, you feel me; I put that on the chic; her momma was good thought I must say, daughter like momma, either one of them was bad I can tell you that boss!

C.J. Moneyway: Ok Ike, you messed around with a daughter and mother combo; so what that makes you the man? Player, you killed an innocent woman for no reason at all. Tell us Ike how was your life coming up, that led you to a life of crime and to use women the way you were allegedly using Táchira. How do your parents feel about your lifestyle, and the man you became in life?

Ike brown: man, I grew up in the projects bro; y'all can't imagine how I grew up and the life I lived. I had 9 brothers and 3 sisters, and we all have different fathers; my dad hustled on the corner right by our building, but still I didn't know my father until about 2-years before he got killed and I was 16-years-old at the time, but I used to see him every day and he never spoke a word to me, until one day one of my older brothers told me who my father was and I stepped to him and he acknowledged that he was by father, but in his line of business he didn't have time for any kids and he told me I was born because by mother wanted some drugs and she was turning tricks on the block. 3 of my brothers got killed before the age of 25-years old, and all 3 of my sisters were getting just as much you know what than I was; well not really but you get my point; and 2 of my brothers started stick boxing you know what I'm saying, stick boxing! My sisters were liking what they should had been liking and they were liking what my sisters should had been liking, that's just how it was man. My mother was never at home, and every other week there was another man in our house, my mom did what she did and they were gone, for real. Another one of my brothers is doing life as well, because he killed one of my mother's boyfriends for hitting my mother one day and he was only 18years old at the time, and 40-years-old now, so no, bro. Y'all can judge me and y'all don't know how I was raised; so I did what I thought was the right thing to do; I didn't have any role models growing up, but the guys on the streets; and the only other man that ever showed me loved was my dope fiend uncle strung out on drugs! Everybody used to tell me how much of a player my old man was and how he was the man in these streets, I guess I wanted that, I wanted to show him that he should had been a father to me, I wanted to show him that I was a chip off of the old block. From afar he saw me on the block doing my thing, he never interfered with what I was doing, he was watching from across the street; at times I wanted to put the barrel to his dome and let him know it was real, but hey that was my old man, even if he wasn't a part of my life. I didn't love him, but from how I used to look at him and what others were saying about him, I had respect for his hustle, and when he did get killed at the liquor store across the Avenue. I felt empty like I knew him for real. I really don't have anything to say about my mother, what are you going to say about a woman you really don't know. Man, by mother would leave me and my siblings in the house by ourselves for weeks at a time, so if we were at home by ourselves of course we weren't going to school, so I dropped out of school in the 7th grade and so I worked on my craft, playing women and making money; that was the life I lived, because that was the only life I knew bro. And I put that on the chic!

C.J. Moneyway: Well Ike, I kind of feel for you brother, but that do not justify what you did to Táchira on everything I love, because your life was messed up and you grew up without your mother in your life, you didn't have to make another mother hurt the way you did brother and nothing is real about that brother! Is that sad that your mother had 12 baby daddy's yeah, it is what it is; yeah it's sad that your father used to look at you in your face every day and never acknowledged you, even all that mixed together Ike, does not justify your actions bro. You are a grown man now, and yeah we all might go through some situations when we were younger, some of us come from broken homes, but as men we have to get over things; ok your father wasn't there when you were a child, he didn't show you love, momma didn't show you the love you thought you should had been getting, that was when you were a kid, you are a 30-40 year old man now, so what you're going to go through thing your whole darn life, so stop blaming it on how you were raised, is that what you are going to teach your children, to hate and never forgiven, never put things behind them and move forward. Player regardless of the way you were raised you are blessed to still be here, but many people don't see it that way. Ike, people like you need to let go of that crutch that you keep holding on too, let that go and become a man and stand on your own two feet; as the good word says; he is of age, he can speak for himself! You are a man now, you are accountable for your own deeds, not your parents, whether you believe it or not! So Denise, how did you happen to know Ike, as he is claiming?

Denise Banks: yeah I knew Ike from the streets and he did bring my baby back to me. See back in the day I used to come into contact with Ike through another dealer, I've been knowing Ike since he was something like 16years old, he always thought that he was a pimp or something with his broke butt; when I wanted some good dope I would go to Ike, because he did keep some good stuff and so I used to give him shots for dope. You know, yeah headshots! He used to work for them Westside boys, and they had the good dope, so in order to get the good dope, you had to give good shots and they would look out for you! But that Negro didn't have to kill my daughter, he didn't have to kill my baby! She gave that boy everything, he was walking around in gator shoes he would get from the d, fur coats, he was driving around in brand new cars, and wore new clothes every day, my baby took darn good care of that killer! Ike wasn't no real hustler, he was just somebody that wanted to be in the streets and he knew people; you know his daddy used to be a street guy before he got killed at barney's liquor store on the Avenue, I think lingo was about 32 when he got killed, he got killed over a female of course, yeah I remember lingo he was cool, now he had respect on these streets, and that's why Ike got a pass, that's the only reason that punk got a pass it was because of his daddy; now that negro in went and killed my baby, on my life he lucky he in jail. Z.J., he's lucky, because I would have gotten him pegged and he knows that; I put that on the Avenue. I told her to leave him alone, he was beating on her, he didn't want her to go anywhere, she was giving him money and he was out here with all these other women, driving them around in cars that she was giving him money for; that dirty low down dog, I tried to save her; I tried to save her, I really did! Where did I go wrong G.I, where did I go wrong, why did God take my baby away from me, I was just getting to know her again, I loved my daughter, I loved that little girl. She went through so much, she didn't deserve to die like that, I will never forgive him for what he did; never! And I don't care what people say, or what they say God has to say, I will never forgive that coward, because he killed by baby.

C.J. Moneyway: Three weeks after this interview, around the same time that Denise Banks got the money that her daughter left her, she was going around the Avenue. Telling everyone how blessed she was and she was spending a lot of money on dope go figure; and one night she went to the wrong dope house; because on December 31st 2015, 3-months to the date that her daughter Táchira Banks got killed. Denise was found dead and naked inside of a well-known dope house on the Avenue, with 2 gunshot wounds to the head, her killers are still at large and at the time of Denise death, she had only $5000 in cash at her house. No one knows what happened to the rest of the money that she had gotten from her daughter's life insurance policy. The money she had gotten from the inheritance her daughter left her.

Ike Brown: Darn shame what happened to Denise; well you can't go around telling people that you would have me pegged, should had thought about that before she spoke it; I'm considered an OG out there on them streets you feel me; and yeah I used whoop that head up on her daughter I sure did, and she deserved it every time I did it too, sometimes a man got to do what he got to do, and if you got to put your hands on your woman to keep her in line, than that's what has to be done I put that on the chic! It was her fault; she saved up all that money and then she went and called her deadbeat daddy, like he really was going to look out for her, who you think killed her momma! I know where the rest of that money at; yeah Billy O'Neill; you don't mess with a guy like that, the man got connections, and entirely too much juice in the state of chic town; yeah when she wanted to open up that big shop downtown, who do think got her the plug for that shop, on a building like that 20-25,000 square feet, 3 stories, who do you think helped her with her business planning, how do you think she got $25million in funding from 5 angel investors who was paid double their investment in a 2year period; look dog, and you just don't become worth over $200 million in 9years without having someone doing some crooked deals for you. Trust me C.J., Billy is the most crooked prosecutor/businessman in the world, believe that player! If T.T. had $200k for the building; he got 5 investors and got over $25million in less than a year, you better know he pocketed $5million of that and have T.T. Pay it back without her even knowing about it, trust me; how do you think we were getting 100 cars a day on the lot and selling about a 100 cars a day, and the lot kept refilling itself, every day; man Billy had the hook-up, he was getting the cars for a little or nothing and we were selling brand new cars to nothing but drug dealers and entertainers for the dirt, a 2013 jaguar getting it for $25k and selling it all cash for $65,000; we only dealt with cash customers that was just the way it was; I was getting my cut and Billy was getting his cut, and T.T. Would see whatever she saw, she had so much going on, she didn't know how much money she was really bringing in you feel me, and Billy had his hands in all the pots, he was getting about $500k a month off the top, man, you guys don't know the real I'm telling you. T.T. By the age of 40 would have been a billionaire and I put that on the chic. You think Billy wasn't watching her from afar, when she had the whole Westside sewed up doing hair in a basement, you don't think that he knew she had that type of money in her bank account at the age of 20, come on man, he was the state prosecutor he knew everything. So when he got that call from

T.T. It was on and popping; quickly he became was her manager, her financial advisor, her model agent, yeah man he had the knowhow and T.T. Started trusting him because the money was coming in, and it was coming in by the brink loads, you feel me; it was on when that first $25million came through that started the trust there. Look C.J., T.T. Was worth over $500 million dollars when I killed her, with the shops and the school, with all her celebrity connections, man, Billy had T.T. Money invested in all kind of things, Billy was making all kinds of secret investments under another company for himself, and it was called YDKN, LLC. Do you know what YDKN means, *You Don't Know Nothing!* Look man, Billy would bring in Bentley's with a 1000-mile or less, he would get them straight from the chop shop for about $40k, I would sell them about 2hours after he would bring them on the lot, anywhere between $150,000- 225,000k cash, that is how we were doing things, and T.T. Thought we were only selling them for about $50k you feel me. Yeah I was making money with Billy, and it was all good, but one day, he figured why cut me in on the profits, so he had me set up, he had 20 kilos placed in my office at the lot and they came and raided the place, and I was the only one that went to jail. You know, and while I was locked up, I was getting word on the street that T.T. was and doing all these hair shows in all parts of the country, word was she was all over the country modeling too, I was hearing that the shop was expanding and growing daily, man the *homies* in the joint was clowning me, no visits and I was finding everything out 2nd hand, she was dating all these different celebrities, and just left me hanging in the joint; and then she called herself, falling for this upcoming NBA player that played of the

Chicago Tide, man please! I wasn't having that, that was my lady and she was out on them streets clowning making me look bad you feel C.J., she was out there doing her thing, while I was in here washing draws and braiding hair; man she had me messed up; so I finally got in touch with one of my real *homies*, that had disappeared in the virgin islands; I told him where I had some money hidden and I finally got out on a $1million cash bond. October 31st I got out of the joint and she wasn't at home, I told her I was coming home, so she should had been there waiting on me, you feel me. But wait a minute guess where she was at; she called herself getting ready to go to the season opener with her friends and sit in some skybox to watch ole boy play ball; that was funny to me, because she must had forgot who I was; so yeah I tore the shop up, and there she was sitting in her office putting on some make-up, looking all good and stuff. You feel me C.J.? I came in and was like yeah baby I'm back why you weren't at home? And she looked at me like, "And!" And I was like who are you trying to get all dolled up for; you know you're not going to that basketball game right? I've been hearing about you out on these streets running around with these guys and you spending my money! What's up! She turned around and told me, that she didn't want me in her life anymore, that she was tired of the beatings and the verbal abuse, and she was in love with this Derik Pose dude, and that she was going to the game, and there was nothing I could do about it! Well there was something I could do about it, she had the game messed up, talking to me like that, she must had forgot who I was, so I told her again to take off her clothes, I was back; I wanted to do the do and I wasn't taking no for an answer. She got up and tried to walk out, I grabbed her by her neck, and started taking off her clothes, she bite me and started crying for help, I barricaded the door and I just shot her in the head; I got nervous after I did it so, I took about $100k she had in a safe in her office and took a Bentley that was on the lot and headed to Texas, I knew some guys there, I was going to flip that $100k lay low and then come back and get that $25million I had in 5 treasure chests at my momma's house but it didn't work out that way and here I am locked up in a Texas prison for murder. Now it's back to washing draws again and braiding hair; see man when guys in the joint see you get played like I did on the streets by a woman, it's not cool, man in here when they hear that you used to put your hands on a woman or a child, let alone killed a woman because of jealousy and you had over $20million laying around and you could had went and found another woman or plenty of them; then you become the woman in these here environments; if I had to do it all over again, I would had treated Táchira with the respect that she deserved, I had a beautiful woman that was all mines, she had everything, good looks and a body to match with plenty of money. I don't know what I was thinking; but whatever it was, it's over now. So who is the big winner out of all of this? You guessed it your man Billy O'Neill, the shop is still going strong $1million a week; the car lot is bumping $1million a week, he got millions in investments, hotels, casinos, apple, face book and just about everything in the chic. I hate that I made him the multibillionaire that he is today; Think about it, if I haven't killed the one whose it really was, and had I been straight up with her from the jump, this would had never happened.

Big daddy: Get off the phone and come here girl!

Ike brown: Here I come, I got to go C.J., my boyfriend is calling me; he wants to go through the backdoor! That's what happens in here! I'm on my way big daddy don't be mad, and please don't be so rough this time, last time I was bleeding for 2days! I got to go!

C.J. Moneyway: Do you feel sorry for him? In the end you get what you put out, and it seems like now he is the one putting out! Now I could probably see how Ike got Táchira in the beginning, a 20year nice looking brother, as the youngsters say nowadays no homo! Messing around with a 15-year-old with social issues, a broken home, and a broken heart, who was looking for someone other than a 70-year-old couple to show her love? I can understand that to some extent. But what I don't understand is, why did she stay in a relationship where she was constantly getting beat on, and assaulted on the regular, why didn't she leave this loser alone a long time ago? Why when she was becoming successful did she keep this guy around? What we as humans, not just women, don't realize is that some people are just in our lives for a season, and after that season is over with you just sometimes have to let people go. See sometimes when a door opens for you, most of the times it is not meant for the person that is with you to go through those same doors, and you wonder why things don't work out; because that season for that relationship was over with, but because you refuse to let go of a no good man or woman, as Táchira if she was still with us would attest to, sometimes you just got to let go! See some women stay with men because they are providing what they want, not what they need, but what they want; you don't need a butt whooping every now and again, but you want the nice house, the nice car, the fancy restaurants, the expensive handbags and the bragging rights that your life is so much better than your friends lives, so you accept the butt whooping that comes along with that; but see Táchira situation was different than most, she was the bread winner, she wasn't married to this clown, she had the 3 story building with every part of it in operation making money regularly, she had the $250,000 contract with the biggest talk show host chic town has ever known. She was the one who was making over $2.5million a month, fashion shows, modeling shows, a successful dealership, plenty of investments generating millions more, she was going to church trying to get her life right with God, and was bringing her mother along with her; may she rest in peace; at this point in her life, Táchira just didn't need a Ike brown in her life, just like many of you don't need some of your Ike brown's in your lives! Get out before it's too late, if I had met Táchira at an earlier time in life, she would had been my wife, and I would had done what the temptations said treated her like a lady. And who knows, she would probably still be here today.

3RD INTERVIEW
(PASTOR) DR. NANA LOVE

C.J. Moneyway: Today on 105.9 the Moneyway Show, we have with us today my friend, my family member (pastor) Dr. Nana Love in the building today who is here to share her both eyes open & both eyes shut experiences from a grown woman perspective; because if you listened to my interview with Denise Banks that I aired on yesterday, but I actually did the interview with her and Ike about 6months ago; I just thought that for Táchira Banks that was a both eyes open & both eyes shut experience, because although she had a big heart and later on in life was trying to move forward with her life without Ike, the fact of the matter is she should had left Ike alone a long time ago that's just how I feel about the situation so moving forward; without further ado I present to you Dr. Nana Love is in the house! Welcome Nana.

Nana: What's going on C.J., I'm happy to be here with you today, so excited that you invited me to your wonder show, the streets are talking C.J. you're doing your thing here at on the Moneyway show and I am so very proud of you. So with that being said I want to give thanks to the head of my life my Lord and savior Jesus Christ, to my husband and my beautiful children and all my sheep at Love More International Church at 7777 Merrillville Road, Merrillville, Indiana 46410.

C.J. Moneyway: So Nana you are a bestselling author with 2 books that has spent weeks on the New York bestsellers list. And I have read both of them and I will tell you they are 2 of the best books that I have ever read: the time is now, and I know where I want to go. In both of these books I can see that you had a story to tell; you know I know you more than most anyway, but these books were still interesting nonetheless. You know NaNa you have inspired me to write a book or 2 and I was wondering if you would help me write and publish a #1 bestseller. Wait a minute NaNa I can hear the hate coming through the radios as we speak. I'll tell you this Moneyway listener; you better start calling those things that are not as if they were. I might not have a #1 seller now but my faith is saying I do have one; see things may be impossible for man, but nothing is impossible for God.

Nana: Listen to you C.J. all I have to say is get ready for your elevation in Christ Jesus. I didn't know until I got here that God gave me a message for you C.J., but first let me address your listeners because you made a good point. Stop looking at your situation as you see it, start seeing God in your situation because if you keep looking at it the way you see you will never see the glory of God in it! We as a people see nothing but negatively in our lives and that is how most of us live. I want that house, but I can't see it I know I will never get that house, by credit is jacked up, by money is funny, and I can't see it getting better anytime soon. Stop seeing yourself living in poverty; call those things that are not as they were and start watching some things start changing in your life. Yeah there are doors that will not open for you without God opening them; there are some places you will not be able to go until God puts himself in your situation. There are things that we can't do period and it don't matter how you try to do it will not happen, because as you said C.J. some things are impossible for man, but nothing is impossible for God; and one reason people don't have what they really desire is because you see God as not being able to do something that you can't do. But God told us that our thoughts are not his thoughts and our ways are not his ways. I know some people think that they are God or Gods, but you're not! 1 day is like a 1000 years to God; how many of you will live to be 1000 years old? You're right none of us, so if we won't walk 1 day with God, how can you consider yourself a God, if we won't walk 1 day with God in the flesh how can I say there is no God! C.J. your time is coming brother be patience. God positioned you with this radio station in order to get your attention for the bigger promise he has for your life. Life is all about steps and order and you had to believe that you could do something bigger than what you though you could do and competing with the likes of the Kings Highway Show; the Steve Harvey morning show and the Ricky Smiley Morning Show is something that you never though you would be doing, but God positioned you, just like he is about to position you to move forward in your next assignment and C.J. I want to tell you that you will never look back again, the greatness that God has instilled in you is beyond anything you could ever dreamed of and trust me my brother in Christ you have always had what is in you, the only thing is God is about to activate the gifts and talents that dwell inside of you. C.J. there are places that you can't go meaning there are places that God won't allow you to go; people that you think love you, people you think that like you or even care about you; many of these people are about to be removed out of your life; C.J. where God is about to take you everybody can't go with you. 1timothy 4(12) let no one despise or think less of you because of your youth, but be an example (pattern) for the believers in speech, in conduct, in love, in faith, and in purity. After today, C.J. your life will never be the same.

C.J. Moneyway: Thank you Pastor Love if the Lord is calling me well I guess I'll be like Isaiah when God said who shall I send and who will go for us; and Isaiah said sent me I'll go. But enough about me Pastor Love, that's talk about you and the life that you lead minister Love; and those two #1 sellers you have on the market. I mean when Oprah has your book on her book club show and not only that, she don't even live life that way. And you know what I mean; I don't want to upset all the Oprah fans so I will leave it at that!

Dr. Love: Now I know this is a family show C.J., but if you want me to tell my story I have to be me and talk the way I feel because that's why my books and my sermons reach people and that's why I have become very successful in both areas of my life. Just like how I try to keep it real with my sheep and readers I will do the same things with your listeners C.J.

C.J. Moneyway: Dr. Love I wouldn't have it any other way!

Dr. Love: C.J. as you read in my books you know that I used to be a lesbian when I was younger, yes (pastor) Dr. Love used to play both sides of the fence. I lived a life that I look back on now and I just thank God for leading me back to him. You know C.J. I hear people talking all the time that God made me this way or God intended for me to be like I am and God is love and if God is love why don't he just respect people loving each other regardless if they are the same sex or not and people were saying this before the same sex marriage law was passed. I mean they are still saying it but people are talking about it a little more forceful and seemed to be convinced that God messed up at their birth and that he made a mistake when he made a woman a woman and a man a man; some feel like he should had made this woman a man and this man should had been born a woman. So in many ways this law that was passed justifies more than just same sex marriages to a lot of people this is a win against God. C.J. I asked the Lord why were so many so-called straight people defending this cause and I'm not even talking about those that were comparing the lesbian or gay movement to the slavery movement that is just out there and I know I will caught some flak later for what I'm saying on live radio but it is what it is! But I asked the Lord, "Why are so many people defending this cause, they are out here saying, 'why everyone tripping they have rights too, they are human?'" I understand that, so I started to ask is it that they have family members that are living this lifestyle, or are they undercover what is it! And one day the Lord spoke to me and said, it is not because they are really for the movement in itself, but it is that anyone that don't believe in me and don't want to live by my commandments they think that this law is a victory against me and that they have won this battle, because something that those who are called by my name are saying is wrong, they are saying that it is right and by passing a law this justifies how many feel, that I am not who I say I am! But they forget or they don't know my true and wonderful servant that these words were spoken in times past; (II Timothy 3:1-5) *"But mark this: there will be terrible times in the last days. (2) People will be lovers of themselves, lovers of money, boastful, proud, abusive, and disobedient to their parents, ungrateful, unholy, (3) without love, unforgiving, slanderous, without self-control, brutal, not lovers of the good, (4) treacherous, rash, conceited, lovers of pleasure rather than lovers of God (5) having a form of Godliness but denying its power. Have nothing to do with such people.* C.J. how can we out smart God when hundreds of years ago he already told us what would be taking place today; how can we think that we are out smarting God as if he didn't know what would be taking place today. Is the thing is he has an answer on how to get out of our mess and the situation we're in, thing is, He has an answer on how to get us out. He knows the way, he is already there and he is trying to show us how to get there; but we want to think that we're smarter than him and the only place that we're going is the place that he in already been and defeated and took the keys away from the enemy; but for some reason that is the very exact place most of us really desire to be! Why because most of us are lovers of pleasure rather than lovers of God.

Now I was living that type of lifestyle when I was 16-years old until I was 36-years of age, so for 20-years I lived that life. And in the process I had my fair share of women, beautiful, educated, paid you name it and I had it except for the what the youngsters call them now hood girls you fill in the word. I had women with nice houses, nice cars that I used to drive around in as if they were mines; had a couple that had nice pockets, I've traveled quite a bit in those 20-years, and up until I got married (husband) did I ever have to pay for a vacation out of my pocket. Look when I was living that lifestyle I loved it. I felt like I was one of the best one to ever to do it; like if one of my male cousins or my brothers or my homeboys would slide up with a nice female I would come back the next day or two no more than a week later I would slide up on them with a nicer one! I was cold with it and if one though it was a game I would come back to the hood with one of their old pieces! That was just me. I had a closet full of kicks with jogging suits to match. I didn't care what people said about me I was living my life; this didn't have anything to do with anybody else. I didn't care how my mother felt; I sure in the heck didn't care about how my daddy felt and to set the record me and my father are very close nowadays he is an assistance pastor at my church. I didn't care about what my grandparents, my uncles, aunts, cousins, my co-workers I didn't care about how any of them felt. I was living the life that Nana Love wanted to live and that was all that mattered! I was living that lifestyle in the 80's and 90's, when people weren't out of the closet or should I say that lifestyle was not accepted as it is today in 2016. That lifestyle in came along way, but it did not just start, this lifestyle started way before any of us were ever thought of believe that! But at the same time this lifestyle that is being portrayed on every TV show that comes on at schools at the work place it aches my heart now that I set these types of examples for little girls that looked up to me back then and I can say now I wasn't a good role model!

C.J. Moneyway: Dr. Love that is cool that you and your father mended your relationship. And I commend you for opening up about your past lifestyle to my listeners today. But why do you feel like you weren't a good role model?

Dr. Love: Because C.J. when God touched me and brought me up out of that mindset and lifestyle about 16-years ago on January 1, 2000; I began seeing things that I never could picture seeing before in my life. I was touched by a spirit and it revealed to me, that all the lives I helped destroyed, all the lives I interfered with, all the hearts and minds that I toyed with over the last 20-years, he told me I had to go back and try to help restore and heal. He showed me all those that looked up to me, all those I lead in the wrong direction I had to get back on track and I knew that it meant I had to go into the wilderness to go and save souls.

Check this out C.J. The first scripture God led me to when it was time for me to come out to begin serving the Lord. (I Peter 4:1) *"So since Christ suffered in the flesh ("for us", for you) arm yourselves with the same thought and purpose (patiently to suffer rather than fail to please God). For whoever has suffered in the flesh (having the mind of Christ) is done with intentional sin he has stopped pleasing himself and the world, and pleases God. (2) So that he can no longer spent the rest of his natural life living by his human appetite and desires, but he lives for God's will. (3) For the time that is past already suffices for doing what the gentiles like to do living as you have done in shameless, insolent, wantonness, in lustful desires, drunkenness, reveling, drinking bouts and abominable, lawless idolatries."*

That was my life C.J. God began talking to me and showing me how I was headed straight to hell; why because of the human appetite I had the worldly appetite I so desired. My human appetites was wanting and desiring and fulfilling any desires of being with someone who had the same thing I have; I desired to touch and be touched by a woman, I desired to hold another woman hand, I desired to look into another woman's eyes, just to kiss a soft pair of lips that's what I craved, that's what I desired, and I felt like God didn't understand me. I felt like why didn't God make me a man at birth since I desired to be with women so much and the more and more I kept deceiving myself into thinking that this lifestyle was right, I just didn't think about it anymore; I just lived it! I was intentionally sinning, intentionally burying and burying myself deeper and deeper in the grave but I wasn't dead yet; I was intentionally ignoring the warning signs of God. I'm sorry C.J., I'm just a talking and talking do you have a question for me?

C.J. Moneyway: Do your thing Dr. Love but what were the signs again that God was showing you?

Dr. Love: Well I don't like opening wounds but in this case I must. In 1992 I had a girlfriend named Rosie and I really loved Rosie and we were together off and on for about 3-years but in 92, Rosie died from a brain tumor, it was said that she had a tumor the size of a grapefruit. I was young plus I had about 2 or 3 other girls I was seeing at the time, but losing Rosie the way I did stuck with me for a while. But by the end of 93 or the beginning of 94 I was just about over what happened to Rosie but I felt like that I would always love her. And then I met her the love of my life at the time I thought I met her in 1995 Rochelle ross she was a red bone with figures like 36-26-38 this was one bad sister she was 6"3" in height mind you I'm only 5"8". Rochelle was a news anchor for ABC Channel 7 news, do you remember her C.J. Rochelle Ross.

C.J. Moneyway: No, I wasn't a big news watcher back in them days Dr. Love; but I just goggled her up and you are right she is a beautiful woman, what happened with you and her?

Dr. Love: Well it was rumored back then that she was running around Chicago with a super star that played for the Chicago bulls in the early 90's. So you got to know that I felt really good about myself when I pulled up on that tall light skinned female at the cheesecake factory. A female that the man, come on the man of the Chicago bulls was known to be escorting this female and now she is my lady, in that realm back then I felt good. Now Roc was one of the sweetie females I had ever met at that time I was getting a little older so worldly I can say that I was maturing in the ways of the world that's how I look at it now. I haven't loved someone like Roc since Rosie had died so that was a new experience for me. Now Roc and I were together from 95 to the latter part of 99. By now you know that roc used to mess around with guys back in the day. Well why I thought that she was all mines she was also seeing this guy from San Francisco named long john now don't ask me why they called the guy long john when he was only 5"7". Now I knew that roc used to go to the bay area but hey she was a top notch professional in the media business and as a part time model so she traveled to many states and cities; but I didn't know that long john was traveling along with her! But it came to pass that at the beginning of 1998, roc was diagnosed with HIV, and how I found out about john was she had to disclose all the partners she has had over the last 5-years. And she hit me with it that she had the HIV virus and she got it from long john who got it from Mary Florence, who got it from Donald Ray, Jr., who got it from a man while in a federal prison in Texas!

C.J. Moneyway: Wow Dr. Love, that was some love triangle that you guys were in, but what happened with you were you affected with the HIV virus.

Dr. Love: By the grace of God C.J. I wasn't in that line of positives. And after Roc died C.J. is when my world got turned upside down; all the human desires I had, the lawless idolatry which were all the things I was putting before God, the women, money, drinking, the smoking, the club life, the excess partying, the lying and the deceit. Now I see a lot of people young women, young men and older men and women for that matter as well C.J. going down the same path I was going down; that same road I was on that same horrible pit where things look like they appear to be good. You know like I got a job, I got a car, I got a roof over my head, and I got a good man or woman or both depending on whom you are talking too nowadays. I got all I need in life why do I have to follow a God who discriminates against people whom he claims to have created. I'm good all I need is *"me and mines,"* and my children other than that I don't need it! All I can say is keep believing that as long as you desire because just like me people are going to continue to live a lie until that lie starts telling the truth! See there are only some things that you will only get from the spiritual realm, some things that you need will not come from the natural realm and if you live your whole live in the natural realm there will be some things that you will never see or be able to obtain. (Ephesians 1:3) *"Blessed be the God and father of our Lord Jesus Christ, who hath blessed us with all spiritual blessings in heavenly places in Christ."* So in order to get to some places in life you have to get to that spiritual realm that is in heavenly places, and those heavenly places don't dwell in sinful places so as long as you dwell in sin you will continue to be out of that realm, many people feel like they don't need to get to that spiritual realm to be blessed because they are already blessed. But I don't know how people think that they know more than God when his word tells us what is required we turn around and look at God like all that is not necessary!

C.J. Moneyway: Pastor Love this passage has been coming to me and coming back to me and I would just like to know what this passage actually means. (Isaiah 6:1) *"In the year that king Uzziah died I saw the Lord sitting upon a throne, high and lifted up, and his train filled the temple."*

Pastor Love: Thank you C.J. that is my confirmation for this visit. C.J. see Rosie and Rochelle were removed out of my life because I had put them at the top of my list of things to worship and things to do, I loved them more than life itself and God saw that he saw that I was putting so much into them and nothing into him. See Uzziah was Isaiah's uncle and Isaiah was very fond of his uncle more than anything, so the scripture said that the year king Uzziah died "i" saw the Lord; and C.J. I'm telling you we will see many things in our lifetime, but there is nothing and I mean nothing is more important than being filled with the holy spirit, do you know in us we have the same holy spirit in us that raised up our Lord and savior Jesus Christ. (Romans 8:11) *"But if the spirit of him that raised up Jesus from the dead dwell in you, he that raised up Christ from the dead shall also quicken your mortal bodies by his spirit that dwells in you."*

There is nothing better when God reveals himself to the Holy Spirit that dwells in you that has been dormant for so long it is a great feeling. And then the Spirit begins telling you that some people in your life have to be removed because he has a greater plan. And he knows how much it hurts to lose someone you love because he as the son watched the son be crucified. But there was something that he wanted to show me C.J.! And what he wanted to show me was himself high and lifted up to see him in all his glory. And for 16-years C.J. my eyes that were once shut are now wide open!

C.J. Moneyway: Thank you pastor love, I truly believe that somebody out there had to hear that not just a part of it but all of it! But in the society we live in today pastor love getting part of a message is better than not getting the message at all. I truly believe that some people had to hear that God removes people out of our lives for a reason. And it don't have to be by death either, sometimes it just seem like people start falling out of your life unexpectedly and some of them that has fallen off you don't even realize that they are gone until someone brings them up! I feel you Pastor Love and Moneyway listeners don't get it twisted, some people in your life can be a hindrance, and then there are others whom we think we love so much and we feel like we can't live without them that we can't let them go no matter what. News flash everybody you meet is not purposed to be in your life forever. So sometimes my people we just have to let go and let God!

Pastor love: C.J. Just always remember this, (Luke 1:37) *"For with God nothing shall be impossible."*

C.J. Moneyway: Thank you Pastor Love for coming and joining us today and sharing your story with us, and I know that you have inspired many today with your testimony and I pray that God will continue to increase you in every area of your life. Remember if you want to hear the true word of God on Tuesday nights at 7 p.m. Bible study and Sunday morning at 11 a.m.; pastor love at love more international church 7777 Merrillville Road, Merrillville, Indiana 46410. Until the next time Moneyway listeners this is your boy C.J. Moneyway saying God bless you and peace!

Chapter 4

YOU NEVER KNOW
UNTIL YOU GET THERE

"What does it profit a man, to gain the whole world, and lose his own soul" (Mark 8:36).

Don't lose your soul trying to gain worldly possessions. So many of us are walking blindly in the sight of God. We don't even know that we are losing our soul daily. There were two guys, one was rich and the one was poor. Now the rich guy would have a big feast daily and would invite his family and friends. Afterward the poor man would come and get crumbs that would fall from the rich man's table. Now it was said that both men died around the same time. It is also said that the rich man went to hell and the poor man went to heaven. The rich man lost his soul, but he gained the world at one point in his life. Wouldn't you like to have a daily feast? One thing I got from this story is that just because you're rich it doesn't guarantee you eternal life. Now don't get me wrong, I'm not saying that all rich people will go to hell or lose their souls. Neither am I saying that all poor people will all go to heaven. This story is more of an example of how material things and wealth can cause people to lose focus on God.

"There was a certain rich man who (habitually) clothed himself in purple and fine linen and "reveled" and feasted and made merry in splendor every day. (20) And at his gate there was (carelessly) dropped down and left a certain utterly destitute man named Lazarus, (reduced to begging) and covered with sores. (21) He (eagerly) desired to be satisfied with what fell from the rich man's table; moreover, the dogs even came and licked his sores. (22) And it occurred that the man (reduced to) begging died and was carried by the angel's to Abraham's bosom. The rich man also died and was buried. (23) And in hades (hell) (the realm of the dead), being tormented, he lifted up his eyes and

saw Abraham far away, and Lazarus in his bosom. (24) And he cried to out and said, father Abraham, have pity and mercy on me and send Lazarus to dip the tip of his finger in water and cool my tongue, for I am in anguish in the this flame. (25) But Abraham said, child, remember that you in your lifetime were fully rewarded with comforts and delights and Lazarus in like manner the discomforts and distresses, but now he is comforted here and you are in anguish. (26) And besides all this, between us and you is a great chasm has been fixed, in order that those who want to pass from this (place) to you may not be able, and no one may pass from there to us. (27) And (the man) said, then, father, I beseech you to send him to my father's house. (28) For I have five brothers, so that he may give solemn testimony and warn them, lest they too come into this place of torment. (29) But Abraham said, they have Moses and the prophets; let them hear and listen to them. (30) But he answered, no father Abraham, but if someone from the dead goes to them, they will repent (change their minds for the better and heartily amend their ways, with abhorrence of their past sins. (31) He said to him, if they do not hear and listen to Moses and the prophets, neither will they be persuaded and convinced and believe (even) if someone should rise from the dead" (Luke 16:19-31).

We can go so many different ways with the subject of forgiveness. We all know people who have committed crimes, even horrible crimes that are forgiven. Regardless of how much we feel that a murder, rape or even child molestation doesn't deserve to be forgiven, we have to remember that you are not the ultimate Judge. I remember a story about this guy named Saul. According to the Bible, he was killing Christians, a murderer of God's people.

He was on a road heading to kill more believers, and then God spoke. There were others around him, but he was the only one that was able to hear what the Lord was saying.

Saul received a name change when God changed his name to Paul. Afterward, Paul wrote more than half of the New Testament of the Bible. So, who are we to judge? We don't know what God has in store for us, let alone for others. Paul is the perfect example of how all men can be forgiven. *"If my people which are called by my name shall humble themselves, and pray, and seek my face, and turn from their wicked ways, then I will hear from heaven, and will forgive their sin and will heal their land. James 4(10) humble yourselves before the Lord, and he will lift you up"* (II Chronicles 7:14).

The key words are "humble yourselves." Too many of us are not living humble lives, we live based on strife, division, and separation. We live for drama. We don't want peace on every side, and we don't understand that the type of lifestyles we're living is wrong. The Bible says that David fought many battles, but when his son Solomon became king he had peace on every side. The reason Solomon had peace is because his father fought his battles for him. We're fighting battles for our children, and they're children. Sometimes people don't know what you're up against because they're not familiar with your battles.

I was watching this show on Netflix. It was about Pablo Escobar. The things that Escobar was doing began bothering me in my spirit! This man was bombing people on street corners; he bombed an airplane, he killed a lot of politicians, and police officers. If you let him tell it he was a good guy, a nice person, a scholar and a gentleman. *"If you do good to those who do good to you, what credit is that to you? For even sinners do the same. (34) "If you lend to those from whom you expect to receive, what credit is that to you? Even sinners lend to sinners in order to receive back the same amount. (35) But love your enemies, and do good, and lend, expecting nothing in return; and your reward will be great, and you will be sons of the most high; for he himself is kind to ungrateful and evil men"* (Luke 6:33-35).

Now there was a part where Pablo's family house had got bombed and his daughter was seriously injured and I was feeling bad for his family. At the same time this was the same thing that he was doing to other people's families. And he did not care. It was a game to him and he had power on earth, even at the beginning of each episode it was written: Pablo Escobar the Lord of Evil. And actually he was a very evil man, he was a child molester, he was 24 and he choose a 13-year-old girl to be with and he married this girl. He was a horrible guy. Now compared to what I said earlier about people being able to be forgiven, well this cannot be the case about Pablo. He died in his sin.

You will have people in this world that love what Pablo did. They would say it's about justice, and he had to do what he had to do. We are living in a sinful world right now and what is right is wrong and what is wrong is right. You shouldn't be surprised by anything that happens nowadays. We have mass killings at colleges and children killing children. Part of our problem is that we idolize to many things and too many people. We look at who they are and how much they have. That is how we based our feelings about any given situation. Life today, is not about right or wrong. We need to get out of this phase of idolizing or idol worship, before it becomes the end of our family.

"Put to death, therefore, whatever belongs to your earthly nature: sexual immorality, impurity, lust, evil desires and greed, which are

idolatry" (Colossians 3:5). *"Dear children, keep away from anything that might take God's place in your hearts"* (I John 5:21).

Stop falling for everything that the enemy is throwing out as bait. Everything that goes out into the atmosphere we take it and run with it. We accept all manner of things not knowing it's not good for us. He says anything that might take God's place in your hearts. Just think about that for a minute. Many people would never put God before their children and that is exactly how the enemy wants us to think. So many people think that they know everything, and that there is no way that God could love their children more than themselves. Furthermore, that lets me know that God is not the head of your life, or you have little faith and lots of growing to do. *"For God so loved the world that he gave his one and only son, that whoever believes in him shall not perish but have eternal life"* (John 3:16).

Would you sacrifice your child for someone else wrongdoings, just because you love them? None of us would probably ever sacrifice our child. To go a step further we don't have Abraham's love, because he was willing to sacrifice his son in obedience to God. God gave his son knowing there would still be some of us that would never be satisfied. He gave his son knowing the sins we would commit. Yet we still act ungrateful and live as though God owes us something!

Instead of trying to be like the rich man, we need to learn a lesson of humility from the poor man. The man that laid outside of the rich man's gate was in poverty. According to a popular cliché, "He didn't have a pot to pea in or a window to throw it out of." His life was reduced to begging and his body was full of sores. Now have you ever seen anyone like that? Most of us would walk pass that person. This man yearned to have what fell from the rich man's table. Dogs came and licked his sores. In order to get a better understanding, you have to know what they are talking about in regards to the dogs licking his sores.

In some other verses dogs were referred to as unbelievers and gentiles. So maybe unbelievers, like many of us are today surrounded Lazarus. Dogs and many other animals have antiseptic qualities in their saliva that humans do not have. So, while the dogs will probably enjoy the activity, the one being licked might benefit in such a situation too.

The rich man didn't realize that he didn't want to go to hell until he got there. In fact, I'm sure he gave it no consideration. See that is how many of us live our lives today. We live as though we don't care about going to hell when we die! We expect God to understand our inappropriate lifestyle, yet we seldom try to understand the ways of God! I never really thought that I would go to hell for my actions; because I was always a good person. I love my children. I paid my taxes. I obeyed my parents. I love my family and friends. Now don't get me wrong, Lord I know I drank, I smoked, I gambled, and I lied from time to time, but only little white lies. I didn't go to church, didn't believe in the pastors that were all crooks, and I didn't want to give crooks my money willingly. I know you understand Lord. I was told that all I need to do was to have a personal relationship with you. With that being said, I thought if I prayed every now and then, I was building a relationship. Regardless of how I choose to live I thought you loved me.

Had I known better, perhaps I would have done better. I would have gone to church. I would have loved people more genuinely. I would have done what was required of me. Please Lord, give me another chance even in death. And all I can hear is when Jesus told the young man to follow him. The young man said, Jesus let me go and bury my father first, and then I will follow you. Jesus replied, *"Let the dead bury the dead"* God is a God of the living! Lord, I let the enemy trick me in believing that you weren't real, although you said that the heavens and earth shall pass away but your word shall remain forever. Please listen Lord, I raised my children the same way I lived, I raised them not to go to church, and not to give the preacher their money. This was the topic in my household, please Lord can I go back and tell them differently that this isn't a place that they want to be.

Chapter 5

THE NEW BEGINNING

"However, as it is written: "no eye has seen, no ear has heard, no mind has conceived what God has prepared for those who love him." But God has revealed it to us by his spirit. The spirit searches all things, even the deep things of God" (I Corinthians 2:9-10).

My walk isn't your walk and your walk isn't mine. However, as children of God, we all have a walk. So, let's take a walk! My new beginning started with a walk. I'm just going to put some things out there that God has put on my heart. If we are not in Christ, our fruit will rotten, regardless of how good your fruit looks now! In the beginning, God created all things by speaking a word. On the other hand, mankind is unique, he formed man with His hands, breathes in us the breath of life, and then places His word in our hearts. God's word lives in me. *"So is my word that goes out from my mouth; it will not return to me empty, but will accomplish what I desire and achieve the purpose for which I sent it* (Isaiah 55:11).

Let's walk through (Genesis 1:1) *"In the beginning God created the heavens and the earth."* Everyone has his or her own interpretation of how many years the earth has been here. Whose calculation is going to pinpoint God's creation? Precisely, no one! No mind has conceived what God has prepared. Did not God create the heavens and the earth while everything was void? Nothing and no one was here to validate God, because He needs no validation. He told job, "Where were you when I created the world."

In the beginning was the word, and the word was with God, and the word was God. (2) He was with God in the beginning (John 1:1-2). Just think about this, the Son of God came into the world as Jesus, a baby crying just like you and I. He was held and taught how to walk just like us. He was loved. At the same time He came with the Spirit of God in him.

Was I always a God-fearing man, of course not! Trials and tribulations changed me. A walk through the fiery furnace made me believe. Did I know things 10-years ago that I know now? Nope, can't say I did! Did I know that in the beginning was the Word? Did I know the word was God? I didn't know any of these things. All the things I didn't care about in my past life, I care about now. The Spirit has revealed to me that God is the beginning and the end.

In this walk of mine, I don't know where he is leading me, but I do know God has taken me from where I was! The word "God" is a title men use to describe the one Supreme Being. He is worshipped as the only one wise enough and strong enough to create and maintain the universe. *"Acknowledge and take to heart this day that the Lord is God in heaven above and on the earth below. There is no other"* (Deuteronomy 4:39). I had to get out of the thought process of mentally identifying super stars as gods, especially athletes in my case. I used to prefer watching a basketball or football game rather than reading my Bible.

Sports isn't the problem, needing to spent more time with God than watching a game is my issue. God provides answers to issues. He's satisfies our intellects and inspire our hearts. *"I have not spoken in secret, from somewhere in a land of darkness; I have not said to Jacob's descendants, 'seek me in vain.' I, the Lord, speak the truth; I declare what is right"* (Isaiah 45:19). With this debut book, *Both Eyes Open and Both Eyes Shut*, I had no idea that God was speaking to me. My heart was shut. Initially, I was trying to serve two masters. *"No one can serve two masters. Either he will hate the one and love the other, or will be devoted to the one and despise the other. You cannot serve both God and money"* (Matthew 6:24). I've decided that either I accept His word as truth or not; either I'm going to depend on my job or God. I made up my mind that I'm going to depend on every word that God says. I've discovered the hard way that you can't do both! Just look at this generation, youth are trying to get rich selling drugs, and professional ball players getting into involved in illegal scandals. I've been there and done that. Look at the churches during mid-week Bible study, and then look at the casinos. Both venues take place on the same night, but people are drawn to sin. What about you? Where are you at during peak hours of the week; at the bar, at the clubs, at home chilling with your special someone; or in the streets just doing whatever?

My point is we need to become more concerned about God. God is not a Jennie in the bottle, He's not an attack dog, and He's not a winning lottery ticket. God is sovereign. And as much as some people try to avoid Him, God sees all things. *"The eyes of the Lord are everywhere, keeping watch on the wicked and the good"* (Proverbs 15:3). I had to realize that I wasn't doing anything new under the sun.

No man can come to God unless God draws him. Parents and preachers can only lead you so far, because they can't give you eternal life. God has lived in all of our tomorrows, as he has lived in all of our yesterdays. *"Remember the former things, those of long ago; I am God, and there is no other; I am God, and there is no other; I am God, and there is none like me. I make known the end from the beginning, for ancient times, what is still to come* (Isaiah 46:9-10). My purpose will stand.

We are truly living in the end times. *"You will hear of wars and rumors of wars, but see to it that you are not alarmed. Such things must happen, but the end is still to come"* (Matthew 24:6). All these things are going on around us today.

According to Matthew 16:4, *"A wicked and adulterous generation looks for a miraculous sign, but none will be given it except the sign of Jonah."* Keep walking… *"No one knows about that day or hour, not even the angels in heaven, nor the son, but only the father. (37) As it was in the days of Noah, so it will be at the coming of the son of man. (38) For in the days before the flood, people were eating and drinking, marrying and giving in marriage, up to the day Noah entered the ark; (39) and they knew nothing about what would happen until the flood came and took them all away"* (Matthew 24:36-39). God has already said that we won't know the time or the hour which he would come, so to me that means at all times we must be ready.

Noah was a righteous man whom the Lord found favor, He choose Noah out of all the men on earth because Noah was upright in righteousness and all the rest of the people on earth were wicked and it displeased God to the point that he never wished he created man. God is holy and there is no sin that can ever be found in God. Noah is a representation of the importance of living for God during times of an unexpected season. The more I read about the children of Israel the more I think about us as a whole. People today, are always mumbling and complaining, never satisfied with what the Lord has done for us. We are seldom thankful for where he has brought us. We always feel as though this is His job to supply our wants and needs. The bad thing about it is, we don't even know how to give a simple "thank you."

Consider how God used Moses to bring the Israelites up out of Egypt. *"I have seen these people,"* the Lord said to Moses, *"and they are a stiff-necked people.* But Moses sought the favor of the Lord his

God. "O Lord," he said, *"Why should your anger burn against your people, whom you bought out of Egypt with great power and a mighty hand?"* That's all we do is complain, just like them, and at times we're so blind we don't even know it's someone standing in the gap praying for us. The only reason some of us are still here, start praying for someone today, you just might save a life from being condemned, and you might even start realizing how powerful the words that comes out of the mouth are!

I feel like walking some more come and walk with me! (Ephesians 6:12) *"For our struggle is not against flesh and blood, but against the rulers, against the authorities, against the powers of this dark world and against the spiritual forces of evil in the heavenly realms.* To me this means that the things we wrestle against in our lives are the things we can't see. Disobedience is an area that I personally wrestle with, not doing what I know is right to God, and continually doing what I know is wrong. But this time I got it right; I obeyed God, despite my insecurities and inabilities. I wrote these words that you're reading today. And God changed my title from writer to author.

People who have *Both Eyes Open and Both Eyes Shut* didn't just start in this generation. Spiritual blindness started ages ago. Spiritual blindness is continuing to spread in the worse kind of way. Sin sick souls have become an epidemic. However, my overall message is God is all-powerful. So, pray that He will open the minds of people everywhere, despite their sinful background.

REFERENCES:

NIV Bible, Amp. Bible, King James
Henry Makow.com/ Rap Music Balant Satanism 8-6-12
Bossip.com/ Deadbeat Royalty: 10 Famous Rappers and Athletes who owe Child Support 6-12-13

www.ingramcontent.com/pod-product-compliance
Lightning Source LLC
LaVergne TN
LVHW021524080426
835509LV00018B/2641